Alpha Nu Society
purchased
Dec 21st/1853

BOSTON, 135 WASHINGTON STREET,
SEPTEMBER, 1853.

NEW BOOKS AND NEW EDITIONS

PUBLISHED BY

TICKNOR, REED, AND FIELDS.

THOMAS DE QUINCEY'S WRITINGS.

CONFESSIONS OF AN ENGLISH OPIUM-EATER, AND SUSPIRIA DE PROFUNDIS. With Portrait. Price 75 cents.

BIOGRAPHICAL ESSAYS. Price 75 cents.

MISCELLANEOUS ESSAYS. Price 75 cents.

THE CÆSARS. Price 75 cents.

LIFE AND MANNERS. Price 75 cents.

LITERARY REMINISCENCES. 2 Vols. Price $1.50.

NARRATIVE AND MISCELLANEOUS PAPERS. 2 Vols. Price $1.50.

ESSAYS ON THE POETS, &c. 1 vol. 16mo. 75 cents.

HISTORICAL AND CRITICAL ESSAYS. 2 vols. Price $1.50.

AUTOBIOGRAPHIC SKETCHES. (Just out.)

ALFRED TENNYSON'S WRITINGS.

POETICAL WORKS. With Portrait. 2 vols. Boards. $1.50.

THE PRINCESS. Boards. Price 50 cents.

IN MEMORIAM. Cloth. Price 75 cents.

BARRY CORNWALL'S WRITINGS.

ENGLISH SONGS AND OTHER SMALL POEMS. Enlarged Edition. Price $1.00.

ESSAYS AND TALES IN PROSE. 2 Vols. Price $1.50.

HENRY W. LONGFELLOW'S WRITINGS.

THE GOLDEN LEGEND. A Poem. Just Published. Price $1.00.

POETICAL WORKS. This edition contains the six Volumes mentioned below. In two volumes. 16mo. Boards. $2.00.

In separate Volumes, each 75 cents.

VOICES OF THE NIGHT.

BALLADS AND OTHER POEMS.

SPANISH STUDENT; A PLAY IN THREE ACTS.

BELFRY OF BRUGES, AND OTHER POEMS.

EVANGELINE; A TALE OF ACADIE.

THE SEASIDE AND THE FIRESIDE.

THE WAIF. A Collection of Poems. Edited by Longfellow.

THE ESTRAY. A Collection of Poems. Edited by Longfellow.

MR. LONGFELLOW'S PROSE WORKS.

HYPERION. A ROMANCE. Price $1.00.

OUTRE-MER. A PILGRIMAGE. Price $1.00.

KAVANAGH. A TALE. Price 75 cents.

Illustrated editions of THE POEMS and HYPERION.

NATHANIEL HAWTHORNE'S WRITINGS.

TWICE-TOLD TALES. Two Volumes. Price $1.50.

THE SCARLET LETTER. Price 75 cents.

THE HOUSE OF THE SEVEN GABLES. Price $1.00.

THE SNOW IMAGE, AND OTHER TWICE-TOLD TALES. Price 75 cents.

THE BLITHEDALE ROMANCE. Price 75 cents.

TRUE STORIES FROM HISTORY AND BIOGRAPHY. With four fine Engravings. Price 75 cents.

A WONDER-BOOK FOR GIRLS AND BOYS. With seven fine Engravings. Price 75 cents.

TANGLEWOOD TALES. Another 'Wonder-Book.' (Just out.) Price 88 cents.

JOHN G. WHITTIER'S WRITINGS.

OLD PORTRAITS AND MOD. SKETCHES. Price 75 cents.

MARGARET SMITH'S JOURNAL. Price 75 cents.

SONGS OF LABOR, AND OTHER POEMS. Boards. 50 cts.

THE CHAPEL OF THE HERMITS. Cloth. 50 cents.

JAMES RUSSELL LOWELL'S WRITINGS.

COMPLETE POETICAL WORKS. Revised, with Additions. In two volumes, 16mo. Cloth. Price $1.50.

SIR LAUNFAL. New Edition. Price 25 cents.

THE BIGLOW PAPERS. A New Edition. Price 63 cents

EDWIN P. WHIPPLE'S WRITINGS.

ESSAYS AND REVIEWS. 2 Vols. Price $2.00.

LECTURES ON SUBJECTS CONNECTED WITH LITERATURE AND LIFE. Price 63 cents.

WASHINGTON AND THE REVOLUTION. Price 20 cts.

OLIVER WENDELL HOLMES'S WRITINGS.

POETICAL WORKS. With fine Portrait. Boards. $1.00.

ASTRÆA. Fancy paper. Price 25 cents.

GRACE GREENWOOD'S WRITINGS.

GREENWOOD LEAVES. 1st & 2d Series. $1.25 each.

POETICAL WORKS. With fine Portrait. Price 75 cents.

HISTORY OF MY PETS. With six fine Engravings. Scarlet cloth. Price 50 cents.

RECOLLECTIONS OF MY CHILDHOOD. With six fine Engravings. Scarlet cloth. Price 50 cents.

MRS. JUDSON'S WRITINGS.

ALDERBROOK. By Fanny Forester. 2 Vols. Price $1.75.

THE KATHAYAN SLAVE, AND OTHER PAPERS. 1 vol. Price 63 cents.

HENRY GILES'S WRITINGS.

LECTURES, ESSAYS, AND MISCELLANEOUS WRITINGS. 2 Vols. Price $1.50.

DISCOURSES ON LIFE. Price 75 cents.

R. H. STODDARD'S WRITINGS.

POEMS. Cloth. Price 63 cents.

ADVENTURES IN FAIRY LAND. Just out. 75 cents.

WILLIAM MOTHERWELL'S WRITINGS.

POEMS, NARRATIVE AND LYRICAL. New Ed. $1.25.

POSTHUMOUS POEMS. Boards. Price 50 cents.

MINSTRELSY, ANC. AND MOD. 2 Vols. Boards. $1.50.

GOETHE'S WRITINGS.

WILHELM MEISTER. Translated by Thomas Carlyle. 2 Vols. Price $2.50.

GOETHE'S FAUST. Translated by Hayward. Price 75 cts.

MRS. CROSLAND'S WRITINGS.

LYDIA: A WOMAN'S BOOK. Cloth. 75 cents.

ENGLISH TALES AND SKETCHES. Cloth. $1.00.

MISCELLANEOUS.

GEORGE S. HILLARD. SIX MONTHS IN ITALY. 2 vols. 16mo. Price $2.50.

ALEXANDER SMITH'S POEMS. 1 vol. 16mo. Cloth. Price 63 cents.

NOTES FROM LIFE. By Henry Taylor, author of 'Phillip Van Artevelde.' 1 vol. 16mo. Cloth. Price 63 cents.

THALATTA: A Book for the Sea-Side. 1 vol. 16mo. Cloth. Price 75 cents.

OUR VILLAGE. By Mary Russell Mitford. Illustrated. 2 vols. 16mo. Cloth. Price $2.50.

CHARLES MACKAY'S POEMS. 1 Vol. Cloth. Price $1.00.

ROBERT BROWNING'S Poetical Works. 2 Vols. $2.00.

HENRY ALFORD'S POEMS. Just out. Price $1.25.

RICHARD MONCKTON MILNES. Poems of Many Years. Boards. Price 75 cents.

CHARLES SPRAGUE. Poetical and Prose Writings. With fine Portrait. Boards. Price 75 cents.

BAYARD TAYLOR. Poems. Cloth. Price 63 cents.

HENRY T. TUCKERMAN. Poems. Cloth. Price 75 cents.

JOHN G. SAXE. Poems. With Portrait. Boards, 63 cents. Cloth, 75 cents.

BOWRING'S MATINS AND VESPERS. Price 50 cents.

REJECTED ADDRESSES. By Horace and James Smith. Boards, Price 50 cents. Cloth, 63 cents.

WARRENIANA. A Companion to the 'Rejected Addresses.' Price 63 cents.

MEMORY AND HOPE. A Book of Poems, referring to Childhood. Cloth. Price $2.00.

JOSEPH T. BUCKINGHAM'S PERSONAL MEMOIRS AND RECOLLECTIONS OF EDITORIAL LIFE. With Portrait. 2 vols. 16mo. Price $1.50.

VILLAGE LIFE IN EGYPT. By the Author of 'Adventures in the Lybian Desert.' 2 vols. 16mo. Price $1.25.

PALISSY THE POTTER. By the Author of 'How to make Home Unhealthy.' 2 vols. 16mo. Price $1.50.

WILLIAM MOUNTFORD. THORPE: A QUIET ENGLISH TOWN, AND HUMAN LIFE THEREIN. 16mo. Price $1.00.

MRS. A. C. LOWELL. THOUGHTS ON THE EDUCATION OF GIRLS. Price 25 cents.

CHARLES SUMNER. ORATIONS AND SPEECHES. 2 Vols. Price $2.50.

GEORGE S. HILLARD. THE DANGERS AND DUTIES OF THE MERCANTILE PROFESSION. Price 25 cents.

HORACE MANN A FEW THOUGHTS FOR A YOUNG MAN. Price 25 cents.

F. W. P. GREENWOOD. SERMONS OF CONSOLATION. $1.00.

HEROINES OF THE MISSIONARY ENTERPRISE. 75 cts.

MEMOIR OF THE BUCKMINSTERS, FATHER AND SON. By Mrs. LEE. Price $1.25.

THE SOLITARY OF JUAN FERNANDEZ. By the Author of Picciola. Price 50 cents.

THE BOSTON BOOK. Price $1.25.

ANGEL-VOICES. Price 38 cents.

SIR ROGER DE COVERLEY. From the 'Spectator.' Price 75 cents.

S. T. WALLIS. SPAIN, HER INSTITUTIONS, POLITICS, AND PUBLIC MEN. Price $1.00.

RUTH, A New Novel by the Author of 'MARY BARTON.' Cheap Edition. Price 38 cents.

LABOR AND LOVE: A TALE OF ENGLISH LIFE. 50 cents.

EACH OF THE ABOVE POEMS AND PROSE WRITINGS, MAY BE HAD IN VARIOUS STYLES OF HANDSOME BINDING.

JUVENILE.

GRACE GREENWOOD'S

HISTORY OF MY PETS. A new and beautiful book, with six fine engravings. Square 16mo. Scarlet cloth, 50 cents.

RECOLLECTIONS OF MY CHILDHOOD. 50 cents.

NATHANIEL HAWTHORNE'S

TRUE STORIES FROM HISTORY AND BIOGRAPHY. With engravings. 16mo. Cloth gilt, 75 cents; cloth, gilt edge, $1.00.

WONDER-BOOK FOR GIRLS AND BOYS. With Engravings 1 vol. 16mo. Cloth gilt, 75 cents; cloth, gilt edge, $1.00.

TANGLEWOOD TALES, ANOTHER WONDER-BOOK. With Engravings. . 1 vol. 16mo. Price 88 cents.

THE DESERT HOME, or, THE ADVENTURES OF A LOST FAMILY IN THE WILDERNESS. By Capt. Mayne Reid. With fine plates, $1.00.

THE BOY HUNTERS. By CAPT. REID. With fine plates. Just published. Price 75 cents.

ADVENTURES IN FAIRY LAND. By R. H. STODDARD. With fine plates. Just out. Price 75 cents.

AUNT EFFIE'S RHYMES. With beautiful Engravings. Just published. 75 cents.

ELIZA BUCKMINSTER LEE. FLORENCE, THE PARISH ORPHAN; and A SKETCH OF THE VILLAGE IN THE LAST CENTURY. 1 vol. 16mo. Cloth, 50 cents; cloth, gilt edge, 63 cents.

MRS. SARAH P. DOUGHTY. THE LITTLE CHILD'S FRIEND. With illustrations. 1 vol. square 16mo. Cloth, 38 cents.

MEMOIRS OF A LONDON DOLL. Written by herself. Edited by Mrs. Fairstair. With engravings. 1 vol. square 16mo. Scarlet cloth, 50 cents; gilt edge, 63 cents.

TALES FROM CATLAND, FOR LITTLE KITTENS. By an OLD TABBY. With engravings. 1 vol. square 16mo. Scarlet cloth, 50 cents; gilt edge, 63 cents.

THE STORY OF AN APPLE. Illustrated by JOHN GILBERT. 1 vol. Square 16mo. Scarlet cloth. Price 50 cents.

THE DOLL AND HER FRIENDS; A Companion to the 'Memoirs of a London Doll.' With illustrations. 1 vol. square 16mo., 50 cents.

JACK HALLIARD. VOYAGES AND ADVENTURES IN THE ARCTIC OCEAN. With Engravings. 16mo. Cloth, 38 cents.

S. G. GOODRICH'S

LAMBERT LILLY'S HISTORY OF THE NEW-ENGLAND STATES. With numerous Engravings. 18mo. Cloth, 38 cts.

LAMBERT LILLY'S HISTORY OF THE MIDDLE STATES. With numerous Engravings. 18mo. Cloth, 38 cents.

LAMBERT LILLY'S HISTORY OF THE SOUTHERN STATES: Virginia, North and South Carolina, and Georgia. With numerous Engravings. 18mo. Cloth, 38 cents.

LAMBERT LILLY'S HISTORY OF THE WESTERN STATES: With numerous Engravings. 18mo. Cloth, 38 cents.

LAMBERT LILLY'S STORY OF THE AMERICAN REVOLUTION. With numerous Engravings. 18mo. Cloth, 38 cents.

THE SAME, in 3 Vols. Red cloth, gilt, $1.88.

PARLEY'S SHORT STORIES FOR LONG NIGHTS. With eight colored Engravings, 16mo. cloth, 50 cents; uncolored Engravings, 40 cents.

PARLEY'S SMALL PICTURE BOOKS. With colored Frontispieces, printed covers. 16mo. Eight kinds, assorted. Per gross,

THE INDESTRUCTIBLE BOOKS FOR CHILDREN. Printed on strong Cloth, expressly prepared. Four kinds, viz.: Alphabet — Primer — Spelling Book — Reading Book. Each 25 cents.

THE FOUR PARTS, Bound in one Cloth volume, 90 Pictures, $1.25.

☞ Any book published by TICKNOR & Co. will be sent by mail, postage free, on receipt of the publication price.

TICKNOR & COMPANY'S stock of Miscellaneous Books is very complete, and they respectfully solicit orders from CITY AND COUNTRY LIBRARIES.

POEMS.

BY

ALEXANDER SMITH.

BOSTON:
TICKNOR, REED, AND FIELDS.
M DCCC LIII.

Stereotyped by
HOBART & ROBBINS,
BOSTON.

CONTENTS.

A LIFE-DRAMA.

SCENE I.

An Antique Room; Midnight.

WALTER,

Reading from a paper on which he has been writing.

As a wild maiden, with love-drinking eyes,
Sees in sweet dreams a beaming Youth of Glory,
And wakes to weep, and ever after sighs
For that bright vision till her hair is hoary;
Even so, alas! is my life's passion story.
For Poesy my heart and pulses beat,
For Poesy my blood runs red and fleet;
As Moses' serpent the Egyptians' swallowed,
One passion eats the rest. My soul is followed

By strong ambition to out-roll a lay,
Whose melody will haunt the world for aye,
Charming it onward on its golden way.

[*Tears the paper, and paces the room with disordered steps.*

O, that my heart was quiet as a grave
Asleep in moonlight!
For, as a torrid sunset boils with gold
Up to the zenith, fierce within my soul
A passion burns from basement to the cope.
Poesy! Poesy! I 'd give to thee,
As passionately, my rich-laden years,
My bubble pleasures, and my awful joys,
As Hero gave her trembling sighs to find
Delicious death on wet Leander's lip.
Bare, bald and tawdry, as a fingered moth,
Is my poor life; but with one smile thou canst
Clothe me with kingdoms. Wilt thou smile on me?
Wilt bid me die for thee? O, fair and cold!
As well may some wild maiden waste her love
Upon the calm front of a marble Jove.
I cannot draw regard of thy great eyes.
I love thee, Poesy! Thou art a rock;
I, a weak wave, would break on thee and die!
There is a deadlier pang than that which beads
With chilly death-drops the o'er-tortured brow,
When one has a big heart and feeble hands,—

A heart to hew his name out upon time,
As on a rock, then in immortalness
To stand on time as on a pedestal;
When hearts beat to this tune, and hands are weak,
We find our aspirations quenched in tears,
The tears of impotence, and self-contempt,
That loathsome weed, up-springing in the heart,
Like nightshade 'mong the ruins of a shrine;
I am so cursed, and wear within my soul
A pang as fierce as Dives, drowsed with wine,
Lipping his leman in luxurious dreams;
Waked by a fiend in hell! ——
'T is not for me, ye Heavens! 't is not for me
To fling a Poem, like a comet, out,
Far-splendoring the sleepy realms of night.
I cannot give men glimpses so divine,
As when, upon a racking night, the wind
Draws the pale curtains of the vapory clouds,
And shows those wonderful, mysterious voids,
Throbbing with stars like pulses. Naught for me
But to creep quietly into my grave;
Or calm and tame the swelling of my heart
With this foul lie, painted as sweet as truth.
That "great and small, weakness and strength, are naught,
That each thing being equal in its sphere,
The May-night glow-worm with its emerald lamp

Is worthy as the mighty moon that drowns
Continents in her white and silent light."
This — this were easy to believe, were I
The planet that doth nightly wash the earth's
Fair sides with moonlight; not the shining worm,
But as I am — beaten, and foiled, and shamed,
The arrow of my soul which I had shot
To bring down Fame, dissolved like shaft of mist,
This painted falsehood, this most damnéd lie,
Freezes me like a fiendish human face,
Its hateful features gathered in a sneer.
O, let me rend this breathing tent of flesh;
Uncoop the soul, — fool, fool, 't were still the same,
'T is the deep soul that 's touched, *it* bears the wound;
And memory doth stick in 't like a knife,
Keeping it wide forever. [*A long pause.*
I am fain
To feed upon the beauty of the moon!
[*Opens the casement.*
Sorrowful moon! seeming so drowned in woe,
A queen, whom some grand battle-day has left
Unkingdomed and a widow, while the stars,
Thy handmaidens, are standing back in awe,
Gazing in silence on thy mighty grief!
All men have loved thee for thy beauty, moon!
Adam has turned from Eve's fair face to thine,
And drank thy beauty with his serene eyes.

Antony once, when seated with his queen,
Worth all the East, a moment gazed at thee:
She struck him on the cheek with jealous hand,
And chiding said, — "Now, by my Egypt's gods,
That pale and squeamish beauty of the night
Has had thine eyes too long; thine eyes are mine!
Alack! there's sorrow in my Antony's face!
Dost think of Rome? I'll make thee, with a kiss,
Richer than Cæsar! Come, I'll crown thy lips."

[*Another pause.*

How tenderly the moon doth fill the night!
Not like the passion that doth fill my soul;
It burns within me like an Indian sun.
A star is trembling on the horizon's verge;
That star shall glow and broaden on the night,
Until it hangs divine and beautiful
In the proud zenith —
Might I so broaden on the skies of fame!
O Fame! Fame! Fame! next grandest word to God!
I seek the look of Fame! Poor fool! — so tries
Some lonely wanderer 'mong the desert sands
By shouts to gain the notice of the Sphynx,
Staring right on with calm eternal eyes.

SCENE II.

A forest. WALTER *sleeping beneath a tree.*

Enter LADY *with a fawn.*

LADY.

HALT! Flora, halt! This race
Has danced my ringlets all about my brows,
And brought my cheeks to bloom. Here will I rest,
And weave a garland for thy dappled neck.
[*Weaves flowers.*
I look, sweet Flora, in thine innocent eyes,
And see in them a meaning and a glee
Fitting this universal summer joy.
Each leaf upon the trees doth shake with joy,
With joy the white clouds navigate the blue,
And, on his painted wings, the butterfly,
Most splendid masker in this carnival,
Floats through the air in joy! Better for man,
Were he and Nature more familiar friends!

His part is worst that touches this base world.
Although the ocean's inmost heart be pure,
Yet the salt fringe that daily licks the shore
Is gross with sand. On, my sweet Flora, on!

[*Rises and approaches* WALTER.

Ha! what is this? A bright and wandered youth,
Thick in the light of his own beauty, sleeps
Like young Apollo, in his golden curls!
At the oak-roots I've seen full many a flower,
But never one so fair. A lovely youth,
With dainty cheeks, and ringlets like a girl,
And slumber-parted lips 't were sweet to kiss!
Ye envious lids! I fain would see his eyes!
Jewels so richly cased as those of his
Must be a sight. So, here's a well-worn book,
From which he drinks such joy as doth a pale
And dim-eyed worker who escapes, in Spring,
The thousand-streeted and smoke-smothered town,
And treads a while the breezy hills of health.

[LADY *opens the book, a slip of paper falls out, she reads.*

The fierce exulting worlds, the motes in rays,
The churlish thistles, scented briers,
The wind-swept blue-bells on the sunny braes,
Down to the central fires,

Exist alike in love. Love is a sea,
  Filling all the abysses dim
Of lornest space, in whose deeps regally
  Suns and their bright broods swim.

This mighty sea of Love, with wondrous tides,
  Is sternly just to sun and grain;
'T is laving at this moment Saturn's sides, —
  'T is in my blood and brain.

All things have something more than barren use;
  There is a scent upon the brier,
A tremulous splendor in the autumn dews,
  Cold morns are fringed with fire;

The clodded earth goes up in sweet-breathed flowers;
  In music dies poor human speech,
And into beauty blow those hearts of ours,
  When Love is born in each.

Life is transfigured in the soft and tender
  Light of Love, as a volume dun
Of rolling smoke becomes a wreathèd splendor
  In the declining sun.

Driven from cities by his restless moods,
  In incense glooms and secret nooks,
A miser o'er his gold — the lover broods
  O'er vague words, earnest looks.

Oft is he startled on the sweetest lip;
  Across his midnight sea of mind
A Thought comes streaming, like a blazing ship
  Upon a mighty wind,

A Terror and a Glory! Shocked with light,
  His boundless being glares aghast;
Then slowly settles down the wonted night,
  All desolate and vast.

Daisies are white upon the church-yard sod,
  Sweet tears the clouds lean down and give.
This world is very lovely. O, my God,
  I thank Thee that I live!

Ringed with his flaming guards of many kinds,
  The proud Sun stoops his golden head,
Gray Eve sobs crazed with grief; to her the winds
  Shriek out, "The Day is dead!"

I gave this beggar Day no alms, this Night
  Has seen nor work accomplished, planned,
Yet this poor Day shall soon in memory's light
  A summer rainbow stand!

There is no evil in this present strife;
  From the shivering Seal's low moans,
Up through the shining tiers and ranks of life,
  To stars upon their thrones,

The seeming ills are Loves in dim disguise;
  Dark moral knots, that pose the seer,
If *we* are lovers, in our wider eyes
  Shall hang, like dew-drops clear.

Ye are my menials, ye thick-crowding years.
  Ha! yet with a triumphant shout
My spirit shall take captive all the spheres,
  And wring their riches out.

God! what a glorious future gleams on me;
  With nobler senses, nobler peers,
I'll wing me through Creation like a bee,
  And taste the gleaming spheres!

While some are trembling o'er the poison-cup,
While some grow lean with care, some weep,
In this luxurious faith I 'll wrap me up,
As in a robe, and sleep.

O, 't is a sleeping Poet! and his verse
Sings like the syren-isles. An opulent Soul
Dropt in my path like a great cup of gold,
All rich and rough with stories of the gods!
Methinks all poets should be gentle, fair,
And ever young, and ever beautiful,
I 'd have all Poets to be like to this, —
Gold-haired and rosy-lipped, to sing of Love.
Love! Love! Old song that Poet ever chanteth,
Of which the listening world is never weary.
Soul is a moon, Love is its loveliest phase.
Alas! to me this Love will never come
Till summer days shall visit dark December.
Woe 's me! 't is very sad, but 't is my doom
To hide a ghastly grief within my heart;
And then to coin my lying cheek to smiles,
Sure, smiles become a victim garlanded!
Hist! he awakes ——

WALTER (*awakening*).

Fair lady, in my dream
Methought I was a weak and lonely bird,

In search of summer wandered on the sea,
Toiling through mists, drenched by the arrowy rain,
Struck by the heartless winds: at last, methought
I came upon an isle in whose sweet air
I dried my feathers, smoothed my ruffled breast,
And skimmed delight from off the waving woods.
Thy coming, lady, reads this dream of mine:
I am the swallow, thou the summer land.

LADY.

Sweet, sweet is flattery to mortal ears,
And, if I drink thy praise too greedily,
My fault I 'll match with grosser instances.
Do not the royal souls that van the world
Hunger for praises? Does not the hero burn
To blow his triumphs in the trumpet's mouth?
And do not poets' brows throb feverous
Till they are cooled with laurels? Therefore, sir,
If such dote more on praise than all the wealth
Of precious-wombéd earth and pearléd mains,
Blame not the cheeks of simple maidenhood.
Fair sir, I am the empress of this wood!
The courtier oaks bow in proud homages,
And shake down o'er my path their golden leaves.
Queen am I of this green and summer realm.
This wood I 've entered oft when all in sheen
The princely Morning walks o'er diamond dews,

And still have lingered, till the vain young Night
Trembles o'er her own beauty in the sea.

WALTER.

And as thou passest some mid-forest glade,
The simple woodman stands amazed, as if
An angel flashed by on his gorgeous wings.

LADY.

I am thine empress. Who and what art thou ?
Art thou Sir Bookworm ? Haunter of old tomes,
Sitting the silent term of stars to watch
Your own thought passing into beauty, like
An earnest mother watching the first smile
Dawning upon her sleeping infant's face,
Until she cannot see it for her tears ?
And when the lark, the laureate of the sun,
Doth climb the east, eager to celebrate
His monarch's crowning, goeth pale to bed, —
Art thou such denizen of book-world, pray ?

WALTER.

Books written when the soul is at spring-tide,
When it is laden like a groaning sky
Before a thunder-storm, are power and gladness,
And majesty and beauty. They seize the reader
As tempests seize a ship, and bear him on

With a wild joy. Some books are drenchéd sands,
On which a great soul's wealth lies all in heaps,
Like a wrecked argosy. What power in books!
They mingle gloom and splendor, as I 've oft,
In thund'rous sunsets, seen the thunder-piles
Seamed with dull fire and fiercest glory-rents.
They awe me to my knees, as if I stood
In presence of a king. They give me tears;
Such glorious tears as Eve's fair daughters shed,
When first they clasped a Son of God, all bright
With burning plumes and splendors of the sky,
In zoning heaven of their milky arms.
How few read books aright! Most souls are shut
By sense from grandeur, as a man who snores
Night-capped and wrapped in blankets to the nose,
Is shut out from the night, which, like a sea,
Breaketh forever on a strand of stars.
Lady, in book-world have I ever dwelt,
This book has domed my being like a sky.

LADY.

And who was its creator?

WALTER.

He was one
Who could not help it, for it was his nature
To blossom into song, as 't is a tree's
To leaf itself in April.

LADY.

Did he love ?

WALTER.

Ay; and he suffered. — His was not that love
That comes on men with their beards. His soul was
rich ;
And this his book unveils it, as the night
Her panting wealth of stars. The world was cold,
And he went down like a lone ship at sea;
And now the fame that scorned him while he lived
Waits on him like a menial. ——
When the dark dumb Earth
Lay on her back and watched the shining stars,
A Soul from its warm body shuddered out
To the dim air and trembled with the cold;
Through the waste air it passed as swift and still
As a dream passes through the lands of sleep,
Till at the very gates of spirit-world
'T was asked by a most worn and earnest shape,
That seemed to tremble on the coming word,
About an orphan Poem, and if yet
A Name was heard on earth.

LADY.

'T is very sad,

And doth remind me of an old, low strain
I used to sing in lap of summers dead,
When I was but a child, and when we played
Like April sunbeams 'mong the meadow-flowers;
Or romped i' the dews with weak complaining lambs;
Or sat in circles on the primrose knolls,
Striving with eager and palm-shaded eyes,
'Mid shouts and silver laughs, who first should catch
The lark, a singing speck, go up the blue.
I'll sing it to thee; 't is a song of One —
(An image slept within his soul's caress,
Like a sweet thought within a Poet's heart
Ere it is born in joy and golden words) —
Of One whose naked soul stood clad in love,
Like a pale martyr in his shirt of fire.
I'll sing it to thee. [LADY *sings.*

In winter when the dismal rain
  Comes down in slanting lines,
And Wind, that grand old harper, smote
  His thunder-harp of pines,

A Poet sat in his antique room,
  His lamp the valley kinged,
'Neath dry crusts of dead tongues he found
  Truth, fresh and golden-winged.

When violets came and woods were green,
And larks did skyward dart,
A Love alit and white did sit
Like an angel on his heart.

From his heart he unclasped his love
Amid the trembling trees,
And sent it to the Lady Blanche
On wingéd poesies.

The Lady Blanche was saintly fair,
Nor proud, but meek her look;
In her hazel eyes her thoughts lay clear
As pebbles in a brook.

Her father's veins ran noble blood,
His hall rose mid the trees;
Like a sunbeam she came and went
'Mong the white cottages.

The peasants thanked her with their tears,
When food and clothes were given, —
"This is a joy," the Lady said,
"Saints cannot taste in Heaven!"

They met — the Poet told his love,
  His hopes, despairs, his pains, —
The Lady with her calm eyes mocked
  The tumult in his veins.

He passed away — a fierce song leapt
  From cloud of his despair,
As lightning, like a bright, wild beast
  Leaps from its thunder-lair.

He poured his frenzy forth in song, —
  Bright heir of tears and praises!
Now resteth that unquiet heart
  Beneath the quiet daisies.

The world is old, — O! very old, —
  The wild winds weep and rave;
The world is old, and gray, and cold,
  Let it drop into its grave!

Our ears, Sir Bookworm, hunger for *thy* song.

WALTER.

I have a strain of a departed bard;

One who was born too late into this world.
A mighty day was past, and he saw naught
But ebbing sunset and the rising stars, —
Still o'er him rose those melancholy stars!
Unknown his childhood, save that he was born
'Mong woodland waters full of silver breaks;
That he grew up 'mong primroses moon-pale
In the hearts of purple hills; that he o'er-ran
Green meadows golden in the level sun,
A bright-haired child; and that, when these he left
To dwell within a monstrous city's heart,
The trees were gazing up into the sky,
Their bare arms stretched in prayer for the snows.
When first we met, his book was six months old,
And eagerly his name was buzzed abroad;
Praises fell thick on him. Men said, "This Dawn
Will widen to a clear and boundless Day;
And when it ripens to a sumptuous west
With a great sunset 't will be closed and crowned."
Lady! he was as far 'bove common men
As a sun-steed, wild-eyed and meteor-maned,
Neighing the reeling stars, is 'bove a hack
With sluggish veins of mud. More tremulous
Than the soft star that in the azure East
Trembles with pity o'er bright bleeding day,
Was his frail soul; I dwelt with him for years;
I was to him but Labrador to Ind;

His pearls were plentier than my pebble-stones.
He was the sun, I was that squab — the earth,
And basked me in his light until he drew
Flowers from my barren sides. O! he was rich,
And I rejoiced upon his shore of pearls,
A weak enamored sea. Once did he say,
" My Friend! a Poet must ere long arise,
And with a regal song sun-crown this age,
As a saint's head is with a halo crowned; —
One, who shall hallow Poetry to God
And to its own high use, for Poetry is
The grandest chariot wherein king-thoughts ride; —
One, who shall fervent grasp the sword of song
As a stern swordsman grasps his keenest blade,
To find the quickest passage to the heart.
A mighty Poet whom this age shall choose
To be its spokesman to all coming times.
In the ripe full-blown season of his soul,
He shall go forward in his spirit's strength,
And grapple with the questions of all time,
And wring from them their meanings. As King Saul
Called up the buried prophet from his grave
To speak his doom, so shall this Poet-king
Call up the dead Past from its awful grave
To tell him of our future. As the air
Doth sphere the world, so shall his heart of love —
Loving mankind, not peoples. As the lake

Reflects the flower, tree, rock, and bending heaven,
Shall he reflect our great humanity;
And as the young Spring breathes with living breath
On a dead branch, till it sprouts fragrantly
Green leaves and sunny flowers, shall he breathe life
Through every theme he touch, making all Beauty
And Poetry forever like the stars."
His words set me on fire; I cried aloud,
"Gods! what a portion to forerun this Soul!"
He grasped my hand, — I looked upon his face, —
A thought struck all the blood into his cheeks,
Like a strong buffet. His great flashing eyes
Burned on mine own. He said, "A grim old king,
Whose blood leapt madly when the trumpets brayed
To joyous battle 'mid a storm of steeds,
Won a rich kingdom on a battle-day;
But in the sunset he was ebbing fast,
Ringed by his weeping lords. His left hand held
His white steed, to the belly splashed with blood,
That seemed to mourn him with its drooping head;
His right, his broken brand; and in his ear
His old victorious banners flap the winds.
He called his faithful herald to his side, —
'Go! tell the dead I come!' With a proud smile,
The warrior with a stab let out his soul,
Which fled and shrieked through all the other world,
'Ye dead! My master comes!' And there was pause

Till the great shade should enter. Like that herald,
Walter, I 'd rush across this waiting world
And cry, '*He* comes!'" Lady, wilt hear the song?
[*Sings.*

In the street, the tide of being, how it surges, how it rolls!
God! what base ignoble faces! God! what bodies wanting souls!
'Mid this stream of human being, banked by houses tall and grim,
Pale I stand this shining morrow with a pant for woodlands dim,
To hear the soft and whispering rain, feel the dewy cool of leaves,
Watch the lightnings dart like swallows round the brooding thunder-eaves,
To lose the sense of whirling streets, 'mong breezy crests of hills,
Skies of larks, and hazy landscapes, with fine threads of silver rills,
Stand with forehead bathed in sunset on a mountain's summer crown,
And look up and watch the shadow of the great night coming down;
One great life in my myriad veins, in leaves, in flowers, in cloudy cars,
Blowing, underfoot, in clover; beating, overhead, in stars!

Once I saw a blissful harvest-moon, but not through forest-leaves;
'T was not whitening o'er a country, costly with the pilèd sheaves;
Rose not o'er the amorous ocean, trembling round his happy isles;
It came circling large and queenly o'er yon roof of smoky tiles,
And I saw it with such feeling, joy in blood, in heart, in brain,
I would give, to call the affluence of that moment back again,
Europe, with her cities, rivers, hills of prey, sheep-sprinkled downs, —
Ay, an hundred sheaves of sceptres! Ay, a planet's gathered crowns!
For with that resplendent harvest-moon, my inmost thoughts were shared
By a bright and shining maiden, hazel-eyed and golden-haired;
One blest hour we sat together in a lone and silent place,
O'er us starry tears were trembling on the mighty midnight's face.
Gradual crept my arm around her, 'gainst my shoulder came her head,
And I could but draw her closer, whilst I tremulously said,

"Passion as it runs grows purer, loses every tinge of clay,
As from Dawn all red and turbid flows the white transparent Day,
And in mingled lives of lovers the array of human ills
Breaks their gentle course to music, as the stones break summer rills."
"You should give the world," she murmured, "such delicious thoughts as these."
"They are fit to line portmanteaus;" "Nay," she whispered, "Memories."
And thereat she looked upon me with a smile so full of grace,
All my blood was in a moment glowing in my ardent face!
Half-blind, I looked up to the host of palpitating stars,
'Gainst my sides my heart was leaping, like a lion 'gainst his bars,
For a thought was born within me, and I said within my mind,
"I will risk all in this moment, I will either lose or find."
"Dost thou love me?" then I whispered; for a minute after this,
I sat and trembled in great blackness — On my lips I felt a kiss; —

Than a rose-leaf's touch 't was lighter, — on her face her
hands she prest,
And a heaven of tears and blushes was deep buried in
my breast.
I could make *her* faith, *my* passion, a wide mark for
scorn and sneers;
I could laugh a hollow laughter but for these hot burst-
ing tears.
In the strong hand of my frenzy, laws and statutes snapt
like reeds,
And furious as a wounded bull I tore at all the creeds;
I rushed into the desert, where I stood with hopeless
eyes,
Glaring on vast desolations, barren sands, and empty
skies!
Soon, a trembling naked figure, to the earth my face was
bowed,
For the curse of God gloomed o'er me like a bursting
thunder-cloud.
Rolled away that fearful darkness, past my weakness,
past my grief,
Washed with bitter tears I sat full in the sunshine of
belief.
Weary eyes are looking eastward, whence the golden
sun upsprings,
Cry the young and fervid spirits, clad with ardor as with
wings,

"Life and Soul make wretched jangling, they should
mingle to one Sire,
As the lovely voices mingle in a holy temple choir.
O! those souls of ours, my brothers! prisoned now in
mortal bars,
Have been riched by growth and travel, by the round of
all the stars.
Soul, alas! is unregarded; Brothers! it is closely
shut:
All unknown as royal Alfred in the Saxon neat-herd's
hut,
In the Dark.house of the Body, cooking victuals, light-
ing fires,
Swelters on the starry stranger, to our nature's base
desires.
From its lips is't any marvel that no revelations
come?
We have wronged it; we do wrong it—'tis majestically
dumb!
God! our souls are aproned waiters! God! our souls are
hired slaves:
Let us hide from Life, my Brothers! let us hide us in
our graves.
O! why stain our holy childhoods? Why sell all for
drinks and meats?
Why degrade, like those old mansions, standing in our
pauper streets,

Lodgings *once* of kings and nobles, silken stirs and
trumpet's din,
Now, where crouch 'mong rags and fever, shapes of
squalor and of sin?"
Like a mist this wail surrounds me; Brothers, hush!
the Lord Christ's hands
Even now are stretched in blessing o'er the sea and o'er
the lands.
Sit not like a mourner, Brother! by the grave of that
dear Past,
Throw the Present! 't is thy servant only when 't is
overcast, —
Give battle to the leaguéd world, if thou 'rt worthy, truly
brave,
Thou shalt make the hardest circumstance a helper or a
slave,
As when thunder wraps the setting sun, he struggles,
glows with ire,
Rifts the gloom with golden furrows, with a hundred
bursts of fire,
Melts the black and thund'rous masses to a sphere of
rosy light,
Then on edge of glowing heaven smiles in triumph on
the night.
Lo! the song of Earth — a maniac's on a black and
dreary road —
Rises up, and swells, and grandeurs, to the loud trium-
phal ode —

Earth casts off a slough of darkness, an eclipse of hell and sin,
In each cycle of her being, as an adder casts her skin;
Lo! I see long blissful ages, when these mammon days are done,
Stretching like a golden evening forward to the setting sun.

He sat one winter 'neath a linden tree
In my bare orchard: "See, my friend," he said,
"The stars among the branches hang like fruit,
So, hopes were thick within me. When I'm gone
The world will like a valuator sit
Upon my soul, and say, 'I was a cloud
That caught its glory from a sunken sun,
And gradual burned into its native gray.'"
On an October eve, 't was his last wish
To see again the mists and golden woods;
Upon his death-bed he was lifted up,
The slumberous sun within the lazy west
With their last gladness filled his dying eyes.
No sooner was he hence than critic-worms
Were swarming on the body of his fame,
And thus they judged the dead: "This Poet was
An April tree whose vermeil-loaded boughs
Promised to Autumn apples juiced and red,
But never came to fruit." "He is to us
But a rich odor, — a faint music-swell."

"Poet he was not in the larger sense;
He could write pearls, but he could never write
A Poem round and perfect as a star."
"Politic i' faith. His most judicious act
Was dying when he did; the next five years
Had fingered all the fine dust from his wings,
And left him poor as we. He died — 't was shrewd!
And came with all his youth and unblown hopes
On the world's heart, and touched it into tears."

LADY.

Would'st thou, too, be a poet?

WALTER.

Lady! ay!
A passion has grown up to be a King,
Ruling my being with as fierce a sway
As the mad sun the prostrate desert sands,
And it is *that.*

LADY.

Hast some great cherished theme?

WALTER.

Lovely in God's eyes, where, in barren space,
Like a rich jewel hangs His universe,
Unwrinkled as a dew-drop, and as fair,

In my poor eyes, my loved and chosen theme
Is lovely as the universe in His.

LADY.

Wilt write of some young wanton of an isle,
Whose beauty so enamored hath the sea,
It clasps it ever in its summer arms,
And wastes itself away on it in kisses?
Or the hot Indes, on whose teeming plains
The seasons four knit in one flowery band
Are dancing ever? Or some older realm?

WALTER.

I will begin in the oldest; far in God.
When all the ages, and all suns, and worlds,
And souls of men and angels, lay in Him
Like unborn forests in an acorn cup.

LADY.

And how wilt thou begin it?

WALTER.

With old words!
With the soliloquy with which God broke
The silence of the dead eternities,
At which most ancient words, O beautiful!
With showery tresses like a child from sleep,

Uprose the splendid-mooned and jewelled night,—
The loveliest born of God.

LADY.

Then your first chorus
Must be the shoutings of the morning stars!
What martial music is to marching men
Should Song be to Humanity. In song
The infant ages born and swathéd are.
A beauteous menial to our wants divine,
A shape celestial tending the dark earth
With light and silver service like the moon,
Is Poesy; ever remember this—
How wilt thou end it?

WALTER.

With God and Silence!
When the great universe subsides in God,
Even as a moment's foam subsides again
Upon the wave that bears it.

LADY.

Why, thy plan
Is wide and daring as a comet's spoom!
And doubtless 't will contain the tale of earth
By way of episode or anecdote.
This precious world which one pale marréd face

Dropt tears upon. This base and beggar world
To your rich soul! O! Mark Antony,
With a fine scorn, did toss your world away
For Cleopatra's lips! — so rich, so poor.

SCENE III.

Antique Room. WALTER *pacing up and down.*

WALTER.

THOU day beyond to-morrow! though my life
Should cease in thee, I 'd dash aside the hours
That intervene to bring thee quicklier here.
Again to meet her in the windy woods!
When last we met she was as marble, calm:
I, with thick-beating heart and sight grown dim,
And leaping pulses and loud-ringing ears,
And tell-tale blood that rushed into my face,
And blabbed the love secreted in my heart.
She must have understood that crimson speech,
And yet she frowned not. No, she never frowned.
I think that I am worthy to be loved.
O, could I lift my heart into her sight,
As an old mountain lifts its martyr's cairn
Into the pure sight of the holy heavens!

Would she but love me, I would live for her!
Were she plain Night I 'd pack her with my stars.
My spirit, Poesy, would be her slave,
'T would rifle for her ocean's secret hoards,
And make her rough with pearls. If Death's pale realms
Contained a gem out-lustring all the world,
I would adventure there, and bring it her.

My inmost being dwells upon her words,
"Wilt trim a verse for me by this night week?
Make it as jubilant as marriage bells;
Or, if it please you, make it doleful sad
As bells that knoll a maiden to her grave,
When the spring earth is sweet in violets,
And it will fit *one* heart, yea, as the cry
Of the lone plover fits a dismal heath."
I 'll write a tale through which my passion runs,
Like honeysuckle through a hedge of June.

A silent isle on which the love-sick sea
Dies with faint kisses and a murmured joy.
In the clear blue the lark hangs like a speck,
And empties his full heart of music-rain
O'er sunny slopes, where tender lambkins bleat,
And new-born rills go laughing to the sea,
O'er woods that smooth down to the southern shore,

Waving in green, as the young breezes blow
O'er the sea sphere all sweet and summer smells.
Not of these years, but by-gone minstrel times,
Of shepherd-days in the young world's sunrise,
Was this warm clime, this quiet land of health,
By gentle pagans filled, whose red blood ran
Healthy and cool as milk, — pure, simple men:
Ah, how unlike the swelterers in towns!
Who ne'er can glad their eyes upon the green
Sunshine-swathed earth; nor hear the singing rills,
Nor feel the breezes in their lifted hair.

A lovely youth, in manhood's very edge,
Lived 'mong these shepherds and their quiet downs;
Tall and blue-eyed, and bright in golden hair,
With half-shut dreamy eyes, sweet earnest eyes
That seemed unoccupied with outward things,
Feeding on something richer! Strangely, oft,
A wildered smile lay on his noble lips.
The sunburnt shepherds stared with awful eyes
As he went past; and timid girls upstole,
With wondering looks, to gaze upon his face,
And on his cataract of golden curls,
Then lonely grew, and went into the woods
To think sweet thoughts, and marvel why they shook
With heart-beat and with tremors when he came,
And in the night he filled their dreams with joy.

But there was one among that soft-voiced band
Who pined away for love of his sweet eyes,
And died among the roses of the spring.
When Eve sat in the dew with closéd lids,
Came gentle maidens bearing forest flowers
To strew upon her green and quiet grave.
They soothed the dead with love-songs low and sweet;
Songs sung of old beneath the purple night,
Songs heard on earth with heart-beat and a blush,
Songs heard in heaven by the breathless stars.

Thought-wrapt, he wandered in the breezy woods
In which the Summer, like a hermit, dwelt.
He laid him down by the old haunted springs,
Up-bubbling 'mid a world of greenery,
Shut-eyed, and dreaming of the fairest shapes
That roam the woods; and when the autumn nights
Were dark and moonless, to the level sands
He would betake him, there to hear, o'er-awed,
The old Sea moaning like a monster pained.

One day he lay within the pleasant woods
On bed of flowers edging a fountain's brim,
And gazed into its heart as if to count
The veined and lucid pebbles one by one,
Up-shining richly through the crystal clear.
Thus lay he many hours, when, lo! he heard

A maiden singing in the woods alone
A sad and tender island melody,
Which made a golden conquest of his soul,
Bringing a sadness sweeter than delight.
As nightingale, embowered in vernal leaves,
Pants out her gladness the luxurious night,
The moon and stars all hanging on her song,
She poured her soul in music. When she ceased,
The charmèd woods and breezes silent stood,
As if all ear to catch her voice again.
Uprose the dreamer from his couch of flowers,
With awful expectation in his look,
And happy tears upon his pallid face,
With eager steps, as if toward a heaven,
He onward went, and, lo! he saw her stand,
Fairer than Dian, in the forest glade.
His footsteps startled her, and quick she turned
Her face, — looks met like swords. He clasped his
hands,
And fell upon his knees; the while there broke
A sudden splendor o'er his yearning face;
'T was a pale prayer in its very self.
"I know thee, lovely maiden!" then he cried;
"I know thee, and of thee I have been told:
Been told by all the roses of the vale,
By hermit streams, by pale sea-setting stars,
And by the roaring of the storm-tost pines;

And I have sought for thee upon the hills,
In dim sweet dreams, on the complacent sea,
When breathless midnight, with her thousand hearts,
Beats to the same love-tune as my own heart.
I 've waited for thee many seasons through,
Seen many autumns shed their yellow leaves
O'er the oak-roots, heard many winters moan
Thorough the leafless forests drearily.
Now am I joyful, as storm-battered dove
That finds a perch in the Hesperides,
For thou art found. Thou, whom I long have sought,
My other self! Our blood, our hearts, our souls,
Shall henceforth mingle in one being, like
The married colors in the bow of heaven.
My soul is like a wide and empty fane;
Sit thou in 't like a god, O maid divine!
With worship and religion 't will be filled.
My soul is empty, lorn, and hungry space;
Leap thou into it like a new-born star,
And 't will o'erflow with splendor and with bliss.
More music! music! music! maid divine!
My hungry senses, like a finch's brood,
Are all a-gape. O feed them, maid divine!
Feed, feed my hungry soul with melodies!"
Thus, like a worshipper before a shrine,
He earnest syllabled, and, rising up,
He led that lovely stranger tenderly

Through the green forest toward the burning west.
He never, by the maidens of the isle
Nor by the shepherds, was thereafter seen
'Mong sunrise splendors on the misty hills,
Or stretched at noon by the old haunted wells,
Or by the level sands on autumn nights.

I 've heard that maidens have been won by song.
O Poesy, fine sprite! I 'd bless thee more,
If thou would'st bring that lady's love to me,
Than immortality in twenty worlds.
I 'd rather win her than God's youngest star,
With singing continents and seas of bliss. ——
Thou day beyond to-morrow, haste thee on!

SCENE IV.

The Banks of a River. — WALTER *and the* LADY.

LADY.

THE stream of sunsets?

WALTER.

'T is that loveliest stream.
I 've learned by heart its sweet and devious course
By frequent tracing, as a lover learns
The features of his best-belovéd's face.
In memory it runs, a shining thread,
With sunsets strung upon it thick, like pearls.
From yonder trees I 've seen the western sky
All washed with fire, while, in the midst, the sun
Beat like a pulse, welling at every beat
A spreading wave of light. Where yonder church
Stands up to heaven, as if to intercede
For sinful hamlets scattered at its feet,

I saw the dreariest sight. The sun was down,
And all the west was paved with sullen fire.
I cried, "Behold! the barren beach of hell
At ebb of tide." The ghost of one bright hour
Comes from its grave and stands before me now.
'T was at the close of a long summer day,
As we were sitting on yon grassy slope,
The sunset hung before us like a dream
That shakes a demon in his fiery lair;
The clouds were standing round the setting sun
Like gaping caves, fantastic pinnacles,
Citadels throbbing in their own fierce light,
Tall spires that came and went like spires of flame,
Cliffs quivering with fire-snow, and peaks
Of pilèd gorgeousness, and rocks of fire
A-tilt and poised, bare beaches, crimson seas,
All these were huddled in that dreadful west,
All shook and trembled in unsteadfast light,
And from the centre blazed the angry sun,
Stern as the unlashed eye of God a-glare
O'er evening city with its boom of sin.
I do remember, as we journeyed home
(That dreadful sunset burnt into our brains),
With what a soothing came the naked moon.
She, like a swimmer who has found his ground,
Came rippling up a silver strand of cloud,
And plunged from the other side into the night.

I and that friend, the feeder of my soul,
Did wander up and down these banks for years,
Talking of blessed hopes and holy faiths,
How sin and weeping all should pass away
In the calm sunshine of the earth's old age.
Breezes are blowing in old Chaucer's verse,
'T was here we drank them. Here for hours we hung
O'er the fine pants and trembles of a line.
Oft, standing on a hill's green head, we felt
Breezes of love, and joy, and melody,
Blow through us, as the winds blow through the sky.
Oft with our souls in our eyes all day we fed
On summer landscapes, silver-veined with streams,
O'er which the air hung silent in its joy;
With a great city lying in its smoke,
A monster sleeping in its own thick breath;
And surgy plains of wheat, and ancient woods,
In the calm evenings cawed by clouds of rooks,
Acres of moss, and long black strips of firs,
And sweet cots dropt in green, where children played
To us unheard, till, gradual, all was lost
In distance-haze to a blue rim of hills,
Upon whose heads came down the closing sky.
Beneath the crescent moon on autumn nights
We paced its banks with overflowing hearts,
Discoursing long of great thought-wealthy souls,
And with what spendthrift hands they scatter wide

Their spirit wealth, making mankind their debtors:
Affluent spirits, dropt from the teeming stars,
Who come before their time, are starved, and die,
Like swallows that arrive before the summer.
Or haply talked of dearer personal themes,
Blind guesses at each other's after fate;
Feeling our leaping hearts, we marvelled oft
How they should be unleashed, and have free course
To stretch and strain far down the coming time —
But in our guesses never was the *grave.*

LADY.

The tale! the tale! the tale! As empty halls
Gape for a coming pageant, my fond ears
To take its music are all eager-wide.

WALTER.

Within yon grove of beeches is a well,
I've made a vow to read it only there.

LADY.

As I suppose, by way of recompense,
For quenching thirst on some hot summer day.

WALTER.

Memories grow around it thick as flowers.
That well is loved and haunted by a star.

The live-long day her clear and patient eye
Is open on the soft and bending blue,
Just where she lost her lover in the morn.
But with the night the star creeps o'er the trees
And smiles upon her, and some happy hours
She holds his image in her crystal heart.
Beside that well I read the mighty Bard
Who clad himself with beauty, genius, wealth,
Then flung himself on his own passion-pyre
And was consumed. Beside that lucid well
The whitest lilies grow for many miles.
'T is said that, 'mong the flowers of perished years,
A prince wooed here a lady of the land,
And when with faltering lips he told his love,
Into her proud face leapt her prouder blood;
She struck him blind with scorn, then with an air
As if she wore the crowns of all the world,
She swept right on and left him in the dew.
Again he sat at even with his love,
He sent a song into her haughty ears
To plead for him; — she listened, still he sang.
Tears, drawn by music, were upon her face,
Till on its trembling close, to which she clung
Like dying wretch to life, with a low cry
She flung her arms around him, told her love,
And how she long had loved him, but had kept
It in her heart, like one who has a gem

And hoards it up in some most secret place,
While he who owns it seeks it and with tears,
Won by the sweet omnipotence of song!
He gave her lands; she paid him with herself.
Brow-bound with gold she sat, the fairest thing
Within his sea-washed shores.

LADY.

Most fit reward!
A poet's love should ever thus be paid.

WALTER.

Ha! Dost thou think so?

LADY.

Yes. The tale! the tale!

WALTER.

On balcony, all summer roofed with vines,
A lady half-reclined amid the light,
Golden and green, soft-showering through the leaves,
Silent she sat one-half the silent noon;
At last she sank luxurious in her couch,
Purple and golden-fringéd, like the sun's,
And stretched her white arms on the warméd air,
As if to take some object wherewithal
To ease the empty aching of her heart.

"O, what a weariness of life is mine!"
The lady said, "soothing myself to sleep
With my own lute, floating about the lake
To feed my swans, with naught to stir my blood,
Unless I scold my women thrice a-day.
Unwrought yet in the tapestry of my life
Are princely suitors kneeling evermore.
I, in my beauty, standing in the midst,
Touching them, careless, with most stately eyes,
O, I could love, methinks, with all my soul!
But I see naught to love; naught save some score
Of lisping, curled gallants, with words i' their mouths
Soft as their mothers' milk. O, empty heart!
O, palace, rich and purple-chambered!
When will thy lord come home?

"When the blind morn was groping 'bout the east,
The Earl went trooping forth to chase the stag;
I trust he hath not to the sport he loves
Better than ale-bouts ta'en my cub of Ind,
My sweetest plaything. He is bright and wild
As is a gleaming panther of the hills, —
Lovely as lightning, beautiful as wild!
His sports and laughters are with fierceness edged;
There 's something in his beauty, all untamed,
As I were toying with a naked sword,
Which starts within my veins the blood of-earls.

I fain would have the service of his voice
To kill with music this most languid moon."
She rang a silver bell: with downcast eyes
The tawny nursling of the Indian sun
Stood at her feet. "I prithee, Leopard, sing;
Voice me some stormy song of sword and lance,
Which, rushing upward from a hero's heart,
Straight rose upon a hundred leaguered hills,
Ragged and wild as pyramid of flame.
Or, better, sing some hungry lay of love
Like that you sang me on the eve you told
How poor our English to your Indian darks;
Shaken from odorous hills, what tender smells
Pass like fine pulses through the mellow nights;
The purple ether that embathes the moon,—
Your large round moon, more beautiful than ours;
Your showers of stars, each hanging luminous,
Like golden dew-drops in the Indian air."
"I know a song, born in the heart of love,
Its sweetest sweet, steeped ere the close in tears.
'T was sung into the cold ears of the stars
Beside the murmured margent of the sea.
'T is of two lovers, matched like cymbals fine,
Who, in a moment of luxurious blood,
Their pale lips trembling in the kiss of gods,
Made their lives wine-cups, and then drank them off,
And died with beings full-blown like a rose;

A mighty heart-pant bore them like a wave,
And flung them, flowers, upon the next world's strand.

Night the solemn, night the starry,
'Mong the oak-trees old and gnarry;
  By the sea-shore and the ships,
'Neath the stars I sat with Clari;
Her silken bodice was unlaced,
My arm was trembling round her waist
  I plucked the joys upon her lips;
Joys, though plucked, still grow again!
  Canst thou say the same, old Night?
Ha! thy life is vain.

Night the solemn, night the starry,
O, that death would let me tarry,
  Like a dew-drop on a flower,
Ever on those lips of Clari!
Our beings mellow, then they fall,
Like o'er-ripe peaches from the wall;
  We ripen, drop, and all is o'er;
On the cold grave weeps the rain;
  I weep it should be so, old Night.
Ah! my tears are vain.

Night the solemn, night the starry,
Say, alas! that years should harry

Gloss from life and joys from lips,
Love-lustres from the eyes of Clari!
Moon! that walkest the blue deep,
Like naked maiden in her sleep;
Star! whose pallid splendor dips
In the ghost-waves of the main.
O, ye hear me not! old Night,
My tears and cries are vain."

He ceased to sing; queenly the lady lay,
One white hand hidden in a golden shoal
Of ringlets, reeling down upon her couch,
And heaving on the heavings of her breast,
The while the thoughts rose in her eyes like stars,
Rising and setting in the blue of night.
"I had a cousin once," the lady said,
"Who brooding sat, a melancholy owl,
Among the twilight branches of his thoughts.
He was a rhymer, and great knights he spoiled,
And damsels saved, and giants slew, in verse.
He died in youth; his heart held a dead hope,
As holds the wretched west the sunset's corpse,
Spit on, insulted by the brutal rains.
He went to his grave, nor told what man he was.
He was unlanguaged, like the earnest sea,
Which strives to gain an utterance on the shore,
But ne'er can shape unto the listening hills

The lore it gathered in its awful age;
The crime for which 't is lashed by cruel winds
To shrieks, mad spoomings to the frighted stars;
The thought, pain, grief, within its laboring heart.
To fledge with music wings of heavy noon,
I 'll sing some verses that he sent to me:

Where the west has sunset-bloomed,
Where a hero's heart is tombed,
Where a thunder-cloud has gloomed,

Seen, becomes a part of me.
Flowers and rills live sunnily
In gardens of my memory.

Through its walks and leafy lanes
Float fair shapes 'mong sunlight rains;
Blood is running in their veins.

One, a queenly maiden fair,
Sweepeth past me with an air,
Kings might kneel beneath her stare.

Round her heart, a rosebud free,
Reeled I, like a drunken bee;
Alas! it would not ope to me.

One comes shining like a saint,
But her face I cannot paint,
For mine eyes and blood grow faint.

Eyes are dimmed as by a tear,
Sounds are ringing in mine ear,
I feel only she is here,

That she laugheth where she stands,
That she mocketh with her hands,
I am bound in tighter bands.

Laid 'mong faintest blooms is one,
Singing in the setting sun,
And her song is never done.

She was born 'mong water-mills;
She grew up 'mong flowers and rills,
In the hearts of distant hills.

There, into her being stole
Nature, and imbued the whole,
And illumed her face and soul.

She grew fairer than her peers;
Still her gentle forehead wears
Holy lights of infant years.

Her blue eyes, so mild and meek,
She uplifteth, when I speak,
Lo! the blushes mount her cheek.

Weary I of pride and jest,
In this rich heart I would rest,
Purple and love-linéd nest.

"My dazzling panther of the smoking hills,
When the hot sun hath touched their loads of dew,
What strange eyes had my cousin, who could thus
(For you must know I am the first o' the three
That pace the gardens of his memory)
Prefer before the daughter of great earls
This giglet, shining in her golden hair,
Haunting him like a gleam or happy thought;
Or her, the last, up whose cheeks blushes went
As thick and frequent as the streamers pass
Up cold December nights. True, she might be
A dainty partner in the game of lips,
Sweetening the honeymoon; but what, alas!
When red-hot youth cools down to iron man?
Could her white fingers close a helmet up,
And send her lord unkissed away to field,
Her heart striking with his arm in every blow?
Would joy rush through her spirit like a stream,
When to her lips he came with victory back,

Acclaims and blessings on his head like crowns,
His mouthéd wounds brave trumpets in his praise,
Drawing huge shoals of people, like the moon,
Whose beauty draws the solemn-noiséd seas?
Or would his bright and lovely sanguine-stains
Scare all the coward blood into her heart,
Leaving her cheeks as pale as lily-leaves?
And at his great step would she quail and faint,
And pay his seeking arms with bloodless swoon?
My heart would leap to greet such coming lord,
Eager to meet him, tiptoe on my lips."

"This cousin loved the Lady Constance; did
The Lady Constance love her cousin, too?"

"Ay, as a cousin. He wooed me, Leopard mine,
I speared him with a jest; for there are men
Whose sinews stiffen 'gainst a knitted brow,
Yet are unthreaded, loosened by a sneer,
And their resolve doth pass as doth a wave:
Of this sort was my cousin. I saw him once,
Adown a pleachéd alley, in the sun,
Two gorgeous peacocks pecking from his hand;
At sight of me he first turned red, then pale.
I laughed and said, 'I saw a misery perched
I' the melancholy corners of his mouth,
Like griffins on each side my father's gates.'

And, 'That by sighing he would win my heart,
Somewhere as soon as he could hug the earth,
And crack its golden ribs.' A week the boy
Lived in his sorrow, like a cataract
Unseen, yet sounding through its shrouding mists.
Strange likings, too, this cousin had of mine.
A frail cloud trailing o'er the midnight moon
Was lovelier sight than wounded boar a-foam
Among the yelping dogs. He 'd lie in fields,
And through his fingers watch the changing clouds,
Those playful fancies of the mighty sky,
With deeper interest than a lady's face.
He had no heart to grasp the fleeting hour,
Which, like a thief, steals by with silent foot,
In his closed hand the jewel of a life.
He scarce would match this throned and kingdomed
earth
Against a dew-drop.

"Who 'd leap in the chariot of my heart,
And seize the reins, and wind it to his will,
Must be of other stuff, my cub of Ind:
White honor shall be like a plaything to him,
Borne lightly, a pet falcon on his wrist;
One who can feel the very pulse o' the time,
Instant to act, to plunge into the strife,
And with a strong arm hold the rearing world.

In costly chambers hushed with carpets rich,
Swept by proud beauties in their whistling silks,
Mars' plait shall smooth to sweetness on his brow;
His mighty front whose steel flung back the sun,
When horsed for battle, shall bend above a hand
Laid like a lily in his tawny palm,
With such a grace as takes the gazer's eye.
His voice that shivered the mad trumpet's blare, —
A new-raised standard to the reeling field, —
Shall know to tremble at a lady's ear,
To charm her blood with the fine touch of praise,
And, as she listens, steal away the heart.
If the good gods do grant me such a man,
More would I dote upon his trenchéd brows,
His coal-black hair, proud eyes, and scornful lips,
Than on a gallant curled like Absalom,
Cheeked like Apollo, with his luted voice.

" Canst tell me, Sir Dark-eyes,
Is 't true what these strange-thoughted poets say,
That hearts are tangled in a golden smile?
That brave cheeks pale before a queenly brow?
That mailed knees bend beneath a lighted eye?
That trickling tears are deadlier than swords?
That with our full-mooned beauty we can slave
Spirits that walk time, like the travelling sun,
With sunset glories girt around his loins?

That love can thrive upon such dainty food
As sweet words, showering from a rosy lip,
As sighs, and smiles, and tears, and kisses warm?"
The dark Page lifted up his Indian eyes
To that bright face, and saw it all a-smile;
And then, half grave, half jestingly, he said,—
"The devil fisheth best for souls of men
When his hook is baited with a lovely limb;
Love lights upon the heart, and straight we feel
More worlds of wealth gleam in an upturned eye
Than in the rich heart of the miser sea.
Beauty hath made our greatest manhoods weak.
There have been men who chafed, leapt on their times,
And reined them in as gallants rein their steeds
To curvetings, to show their sweep of limb;
Yet love hath on their broad brows written 'fool.'
Sages, with passions held in leash like hounds,—
Grave Doctors, tilting with a lance of light
In lists of argument,—have knelt and sighed
Most plethoric sighs, and been but very men;
Stern hearts, close barred against a wanton world,
Have had their gates burst open by a kiss.
Why, there was one who might have topped all men,
Who bartered joyously, for a single smile,
This empired planet with its load of crowns,
And thought himself enriched. If ye are fair,
Mankind will crowd around you, thick as when

The full-faced moon sits silver on the sea,
The eager waves lift up their gleaming heads,
Each shouldering for her smile."

The lady dowered him with her richest look,
Her arch head half aside; her liquid eyes
From 'neath their dim lids drooping slumberous,
Stood full on his, and called the wild blood up
All in a tumult to his sun-kissed cheek, —
As if it wished to see her beauty too, —
Then asked in dulcet tones, "Dost think *me* fair?"
"O, thou art fairer than an Indian morn,
Seated in her sheen palace of the east.
Thy faintest smile out-prices the swelled wombs
Of fleets, rich glutted, toiling wearily
To vomit all their wealth on English strands.
The whiteness of this hand should ne'er receive
A poorer greeting than the kiss of kings;
And on thy happy lips doth sit a joy,
Fuller than any gathered by the gods,
In all the rich range of their golden heaven."
"Now, by my mother's white enskied soul!"
The lady cried, 'twixt laugh and blush the while,
"I'll swear *thou 'st* been in love, my Indian sweet.
Thy spirit on another breaks in joy,
Like the pleased sea on a white-breasted shore —
A shore that wears on her alluring brows

Rare shells, far brought, the love-gifts of the sea,
That blushed a tell-tale. Now, I swear by all
The well-washed jewels strewn on fathom sands,
That thou dost keep her looks, her words, her sighs,
Her laughs, her tears, her angers, and her frowns,
Balmed between memory's leaves; and every day
Dost count them o'er and o'er in solitude,
As pious monks count o'er their rosaries.
Now, tell me, did she give thee love for love?
Or didst thou make midnight thy confidant,
Telling her all about thy lady's eyes,
How rich her cheek, how cold as death her scorn?
My lustrous Leopard, hast thou been in love?"
The Page's dark face flushed the hue of wine
In crystal goblet stricken by the sun;
His soul stood like a moon within his eyes,
Suddenly orbed; his passionate voice was shook
By trembles into music. — "Thee I love."
"Thou!" and the Lady, with a cruel laugh
(Each silver throb went through him like a sword),
Flung herself back upon her fringéd couch.
From which she rose upon him like a queen,
She rose and stabbed him with her angry eyes.
"'T is well my father did not hear thee, boy,
Or else my pretty plaything of an hour
Might have gone sleep to-night without his head,
And I might waste rich tears upon his fate.

I would not have my sweetest plaything hurt.
Dost think to scorch me with those blazing eyes,
My fierce and lightning-blooded cub o' the sun?
Thy blood is up in riot on thy brow.
I' the face o' its monarch. Peace! By my gray sire,
Now could I slay thee with one look of hate,
One single look! My Hero! my Heart-god!
My dusk Hyperion, Bacchus of the Inds!
My Hercules, with chin as smooth as my own!
I am so sorry maid, I cannot wear
This great and proffered jewel of thy love.
Thou art too bold, methinks! Didst never fear
That on my poor deserts thy love would sit
Like a great diamond on a threadbare robe?
I tremble for 't. I prithee, come to-morrow
And I will pasture you upon my lips
Until thy beard be grown. Go now, sir, go."
As thence she waved him with arm-sweep superb,
The light of scorn was cold within her eyes,
And withered his bloomed heart, which, like a rose,
Had opened, timid, to the noon of love.

The lady sank again into her couch,
Panting and flushed; slowly she paled with thought;
When she looked up the sun had sunk an hour,
And one round star shook in the orange west.
The lady sighed, "It was my father's blood

That bore me, as a red and wrathful stream
Bears a shed leaf. I would recall my words,
And yet I would not.
Into what angry beauty rushed his face!
What lips! what splendid eyes! 't was pitiful
To see such splendors ebb in utter woe.
His eyes half won me. Tush! I am a fool;
The blood that purples in these azure veins,
Riched with its long course through a hundred earls,
Were fouled and mudded if I stooped to him.
My father loves him for his free wild wit;
I for his beauty and sun-lighted eyes.
To bring him to my feet, to kiss my hand,
Had I it in my gift, I 'd give the world,
Its panting fire-heart, diamonds, veins of gold;
Its rich strands, oceans, belts of cedared hills,
Whence summer smells are struck by all the winds.
But whether I might lance him through the brain
With a proud look, — or whether sternly kill
Him with a single deadly word of scorn, —
Or whether yield me up,
And sink all tears and weakness in his arms,
And strike him blind with a strong shock of joy —
Alas! I feel I could do each and all.
I will be kind when next he brings me flowers,
Plucked from the shining forehead of the morn,
Ere they have oped their rich cores to the bee.

His wild heart with a ringlet will I chain,
And o'er him I will lean me like a heaven,
And feed him with sweet looks and dew-soft words,
And beauty that might make a monarch pale,
And thrill him to the heart's core with a touch;
Smile him to Paradise at close of eve,
To hang upon my lips in silver dreams."

LADY.

What, art thou done already? Thy tale is like
A day unsealed with sunset. What though dusk?
A dusky rod of iron hath power to draw
The lightnings from their heaven to itself.
The richest wage you can pay love — is love.

WALTER.

Then close the tale thyself, — I drop the mask;
I am the sun-tanned Page; the Lady, thou!
I take thy hand, it trembles in my grasp;
I look in thy face and see no frown in it.
O, may my spirit on hope's ladder climb
From hungry nothing up to star-packed space,
Thence strain on tip-toe to thy love beyond —
The only heaven I ask!

LADY.

My God! 't is hard!

When I was all in leaf the frost winds came,
And now, when o'er me runs the summer's breath
It waves but iron boughs.

WALTER.

What dost thou murmur?
Thy cheek burns mad as mine. O untouched lips!
I see them as a glorious rebel sees
A crown within his reach. I'll taste their bliss,
Although the price be death ——

LADY (*springing up*).

Walter! beware!
These tell-tale heavens are listening earnestly.
O Sir! within a month my bridal bells
Will make a village glad. The fainting Earth
Is bleeding at her million golden veins,
And by her blood I'm bought. The sun shall see
A pale bride wedded to gray hair, and eyes
Of cold and cruel blue; and in the spring
A grave with daisies on it.

WALTER.

My world is cracked,
My brittle brilliant world! These knife-like words
Have left a deep red gash across my heart.

LADY.

We twain have met like ships upon the sea,
Who hold an hour's converse, so short, so sweet;
One little hour! and then, away they speed
On lonely paths, through mist, and cloud, and foam,
To meet no more. We have been foolish, Walter!
I would to God that I had never known
This secret of thy heart, or else had met thee
Years before this. I bear a heavy doom.
If thy rich heart is like a palace shattered,
Stand up amid the ruins of thy heart,
And with a calm brow front the solemn stars.

[LADY *pauses;* WALTER *remains silent.*

'T is four o'clock already. See, the moon
Has climbed the blue steep of the eastern sky,
And sits and tarries for the coming night.
So let thy soul be up and ready armed,
In waiting till occasion comes like night;
As night to moons to souls occasion comes.
I am thine elder, WALTER! in the heart.
I read thy future like an open book:
I see thou shalt have grief; I also see
Thy grief's edge blunted on the iron world.
Be brave and strong through all thy wrestling years,
A brave soul is a thing which all things serve;
When the great Corsican from Elba came,
The soldiers sent to take him bound or dead

Were struck to statues by his kingly eyes:
He spoke — they broke their ranks, they clasped his
knees,
With tears along a cheering road of triumph
They bore him to a throne. Know when to die!
Perform thy work and straight return to God.
Be thou the midnight's white and drenching moon;
Set, when the midnight thou hast filled is past.
O! there are men who linger on the stage
To gather crumbs and fragments of applause
When they should sleep in earth — who, like the moon,
Have brightened up some little night of time,
And 'stead of setting when their light is worn,
Still linger, like its blank and beamless orb,
When daylight fills the sky. But I must go.
Nay, nay, I go alone! Yet one word more, —
Strive for the Poet's crown, but ne'er forget
How poor are fancy's blooms to thoughtful fruits;
That gold and crimson mornings, though more bright
Than soft blue days, are scarcely half their worth.
Walter, farewell! the world shall hear of thee.

[LADY *still lingers.*

I have a strange sweet thought. I do believe
I shall be dead in spring, and that the soul
Which animates and doth inform these limbs
Will pass into the daisies of my grave:
If memory shall ever lead thee there,

Through daisies I 'll look up into thy face
And feel a dim sweet joy; and if they move,
As in a little wind, thou 'lt know 't is I. [LADY *goes.*

WALTER (*after a long interval, looking up*).

God! what a light has passed away from earth
Since my last look! How hideous this night!
How beautiful the yesterday that stood
Over me like a rainbow! I am alone.
The past is past. I see the future stretch
All dark and barren as a rainy sea.

SCENE V.

WALTER, *wandering down a rural lane. Evening of the same day as Scene IV.*

WALTER.

SUNSET is burning like the seal of God
Upon the close of day. — This very hour
Night mounts her chariot in the eastern glooms
To chase the flying Sun, whose flight has left
Footprints of glory in the clouded west:
Swift is she haled by wingéd swimming steeds,
Whose cloudy manes are wet with heavy dews,
And dews are drizzling from her chariot-wheels.
Soft in her lap lies drowsy-lidded Sleep,
Brainful of dreams, as summer-hive with bees;
And round her in the pale and spectral light
Flock bats and grisly owls on noiseless wings.
The flying sun goes down the burning west,
Vast night comes noiseless up the eastern slope,
And so the eternal chase goes round the world.

Unrest! unrest! The passion-panting sea
Watches the unveiled beauty of the stars
Like a great hungry soul. The unquiet clouds
Break and dissolve, then gather in a mass,
And float like mighty icebergs through the blue.
Summers, like blushes, sweep the face of earth;
Heaven yearns in stars. Down comes the frantic rain;
We hear the wail of the remorseful winds
In their strange penance. And this wretched orb
Knows not the taste of rest; a maniac world,
Homeless and sobbing through the deep she goes.

[*A Child runs past;* WALTER *looks after her.*

O thou bright thing, fresh from the hand of God!
The motions of thy dancing limbs are swayed
By the unceasing music of thy being!
Nearer I seem to God when looking on thee.
'T is ages since he made his youngest star,
His hand was on thee as 't were yesterday.
Thou later Revelation! Silver Stream,
Breaking with laughter from the lake divine
Whence all things flow! O bright and singing babe!
What wilt thou be hereafter?— Why should man
Perpetuate this round of misery
When he has in his hand the power to close it?
Let there be no warm hearts, no love on earth.
No Love! No Love! Love bringeth wretchedness.
No holy marriage. No sweet infant smiles.

No mother's bending o'er the innocent sleep
With unvoiced prayers and with happy tears.
Let the whole race die out, and with a stroke,
A master-stroke, at once cheat Death and Hell
Of half of their enormous revenues.

[WALTER *approaches a cottage, a peasant sitting at the door.*

One of my peasants. 'T is a fair eve.

PEASANT.

Ay, Master!
How sweet the smell of beans upon the air!
The wheat is earing fairly. We have reason
For thankfulness to God.

WALTER (*looking upward*).

We *have* great reason;
For He provides a balm for all our woes.
He has made Death. Thrice blessed be His name!

PEASANT.

He has made Heaven ——

WALTER.

To yawn eternities.
Did I say Death? O God! there is no death.
When our eyes close, we only pass one stage

Of our eternal being. Your hand, my friend!
For thou and I are sharers in one doom:
We are immortals; and must bear such woe
That, could it light on God, in agony
He 'd pay down all His stars to buy the death
He doth deny us. — Dost thou wish to die?

PEASANT.

I trust in God to live for many years,
Although with a worn frame and with a heart
Somewhat the worse for wear.

WALTER.

O fool! fool! fool!
These hands are brown with toil, that brow is seamed,
Still you must sweat and swelter in the sun,
And trudge, with feet benumbed, the winter's snow,
Nor intermission have until the end.
Thou canst not draw down fame upon thy head,
And yet would cling to life! I 'll not believe it;
The faces of all things belie their hearts,
Each man 's as weary of his life as I.
This anguished earth shines on the moon — a moon.
The moon hides with a cloak of tender light
A scarred heart fed upon by hungry fires.
Black is this world, but blacker is the next;
There is no rest for any living soul:

We are immortals — and must bear with us
Through all eternity this hateful being;
Restlessly flitting from pure star to star,
The memory of our sins, deceits, and crimes,
Will eat into us like a poisoned robe.
Yet thou canst wear content upon thy face
And talk of thankfulness! O die, man, die!
Get underneath the earth for very shame.

[*During this speech the Child draws near; at its close her Father presents her to* WALTER.

Is this thy answer? [*Looks at her earnestly.*
O, my worthy friend,
I lost a world to-day and shed no tear;
Now I could weep for *thee.* Sweet sinless one!
My heart is weak as a great globe, all sea.
It finds no shore to break on but thyself:
So let it break.

[*He hides his face in his hands, the Child looking fearfully up at him.*

SCENE VI.

A Room in London. WALTER *reading from a Manuscript.*

My head is gray, my blood is young,
Red-leaping in my veins,
The spring doth stir my spirit yet
To seek the cloistered violet,
The primrose in the lanes.
In heart I am a very boy,
Haunting the woods, the waterfalls,
The ivies on gray castle-walls;
Weeping in silent joy
When the broad sun goes down the west,
Or trembling o'er a sparrow's nest.
The world might laugh were I to tell
What most my old age cheers, —
Memories of stars and crescent moons,
Of nutting strolls through autumn noons,

Rainbows 'mong April's tears.
But chief, to live that hour again,
When first I stood on sea-beach old,
First heard the voice, first saw out-rolled
The glory of the main.
Many rich draughts hath Memory,
The Soul's cup-bearer, brought to me.

I saw a garden in my strolls,
A lovely place, I ween,
With rows of vermeil-blossomed trees,
With flowers, with slumberous haunts of bees,
With summer-house of green.
A peacock perched upon a dial,
In the sun's face he did unclose
His train superb with eyes and glows,
To dare the sun to trial.
A child sat in a shady place,
A shower of ringlets round her face.

She sat on shaven plot of grass,
With earnest face, and weaving
Lilies white and freakéd pansies
Into quaint delicious fancies,
Then, on a sudden leaving
Her floral wreath, she would upspring
With silver shouts and ardent eyes,
To chase the yellow butterflies,

Making the garden ring;
Then gravely pace the scented walk,
Soothing her doll with childish talk.

And being, as I said before,
An old man who could find
A boundless joy beneath the skies,
And in the light of human eyes,
And in the blowing wind,
There daily were my footsteps turned,
Through the long spring, till autumn's peaches
Were drooping full-juiced in my reaches.—
Each day my old heart yearned
To look upon that child so fair,
That infant in her golden hair.

In this green lovely world of ours
I have had many pets;
Two are still leaping in the sun,
Three are married; *that* dearest one
Is 'neath the violets.
I gazéd till my heart grew wild,
To fold her in my warm caresses,
Clasp her showers of golden tresses,—
O, dreamy-eyéd child!
O Child of Beauty! still thou art
A sunbeam in this lonely heart.

When autumn eves grew chill and rainy,
England left I for the Ganges;
I couched 'mong groves of cedar-trees,
Blue lakes, and slumberous palaces,
Crossed the snows of mountain-ranges,
Watched the set of old Orion,
Saw wild flocks and wild-eyed shepherds,
Princes charioted by leopards,
In the desert met the lion,
The mad sun above us glaring, —
Child! for thee I still was caring.

Home returned from realms barbaric,
By the shores of Loch Lubnaig,
A dear friend and I were walking
('T was the Sabbath), we were talking
Of dreams and feelings vague;
We pausèd by a place of graves,
Scarcely a word was 'twixt us given,
Silent the earth, silent the heaven,
No murmur of the waves,
The awèd Loch lay black and still
In the black shadow of the hill.

We loosed the gate and wandered in,
When the sun eternal
Was sudden blanched with amethyst,
As if a thick and purple mist

Dusked his brows supernal.
Soon, like a god in mortal throes,
City, hill and sea, he dips
In the death-hues of eclipse;
Mightier his anguish grows,
Till he hung black, with ring intense,
The wreck of his magnificence.

Above the earth's cold face he hung
With a pale ring of glory,
Like that which cunning limners paint
Around the forehead of a saint,
Or brow of martyr hoary.
And sitting there I could but choose, —
That blind and stricken sun aboon,
Stars shuddering through the ghostly noon,
'Mong the thick-falling dews, —
To tell, with features pale and wild,
About that Garden and that Child.

When moons had waxed and waned, I stood
Beside the garden-gate,
The Peacock's dial was overthrown,
The walks with moss were overgrown,
Her bower was desolate.
Gazing in utter misery
Upon that sad and silent place,

A woman came with mournful face,
And thus she said to me, —
" Those trees, as they were human souls,
All withered at the death-bell knolls."

I turned and asked her of the child.
" She is gone hence," quoth she,
" To be with Christ in Paradise.
O, sir! I stilled her infant cries,
I nursed her on my knee.
Though we were ever at her side,
And saw life fading in her cheek,
She knew us not, nor did she speak,
Till just before she died;
In the wild heart of that eclipse,
These words came through her wasted lips:

' The callow young were huddling in the nests,
The marigold was burning in the marsh,
Like a thing dipt in sunset, when He came.

My blood went up to meet Him on my face,
Glad as a child that hears its father's step,
And runs to meet him at the open porch.

I gave Him all my being, like a flower
That flings its perfume on a vagrant breeze;
A breeze that wanders on and heeds it not.

His scorn is lying on my heart like snow,
My eyes are weary, and I fain would sleep;
The quietest sleep is underneath the ground

Are ye around me, friends? I cannot see,
I cannot hear the voices that I love,
I lift my hands to you from out the night.

Methought I felt a tear upon my cheek;
Weep not, my mother! It is time to rest,
And I am very weary; so, good-night!'

"My heart is in the grave with her,
The family went abroad;
Last autumn you might see the fruits,
Neglected, rot round the tree-roots;
This spring no leaves they showed.
I sometimes fear my brain is crost;
Around this place, the church-yard yonder,
All day, all night, I silent wander,
As woful as a ghost ——
God take me to His gracious keeping,
But this old man is wildly weeping!"

That night the sky was heaped with clouds;
Through one blue gulf profound,
Begirt with many a cloudy crag,
The moon came rushing like a stag,

And one star like a hound.
Wearily the chase I eyed,
Wearily I saw the Dawn's
Feet sheening o'er the dewy lawns.
O God! that I had died.
My heart's red tendrils were all torn
And bleeding on that summer morn.

WALTER (*after a long silence, speaking abstractedly, and with frequent pauses*).

Twice hath the windy summer made a noise
Of leaves o'er all the land from sea to sea,
And still that Child's face sleeps within my heart
Like a young sunbeam in a gloomy wood,
Making the darkness smile — I almost smile
At the strange fancies I have girt her with;
The garden, peacock, and the black eclipse,
The still old grave-yard 'mong the dreary hills,
Gray mourners round it — I wonder if she 's dead?
She was too fair for earth. Ah! she would die
Like music, sunbeams, and the pallid flowers
That spring on Winter's corse — I saw those graves
With Him who is no more. They are all dead,
The beings whom I loved, and I am sad,
But would not change my sadness for a life
Without a fissure running through its joy.
This very hour a suite of sumptuous rooms

O'erflows with music like a cup with wine;
Outside, the night is weeping like a girl
At her seducer's door, and still the rooms
Run o'er with music, careless of her woe.
I would not have my heart thus. This poor rhyme
Is but an adumbration of my life,
My misery tricked out in a quaint disguise.
O, it did happen on a summer day,
When I was playing unawares with flowers,
That happiness shot past me like a planet,
And I was barren left!

Enter EDWARD (*unobserved*).

EDWARD.

Walter 's love-sick for Fame:
A haughty mistress! How this mad old world
Reels to its burning grave, shouting forth names,
Like a wild drunkard at his frenzy's height,
And they who bear them deem such shoutings *Fame*,
And, smiling, die content. What is thy thought?

WALTER.

'T is this, a sad one: — Though our beings point
Upward, like prayers or quick spires of flame,
We soon lose interest in this breathing world.
Joy palls from taste to taste, until we yawn

In Pleasure's glowing face. When first we love,
Our souls are clad with joy, as if a tree,
All winter-bare, had on a sudden leapt
To a full load of blooms; next time 't is naught.
Great weariness doth feed upon the soul;
(I sometimes think the highest-blest in heaven
Will weary 'mong its flowers.) As for myself,
There 's nothing new between me and the grave
But the cold feel of Death.

EDWARD.

Watch well thy heart!
It is, methinks, an eager shaking star,
Not a calm steady planet.

WALTER.

I love thee much,
But thou art all unlike the glorious guide
Of my proud boyhood. O, he led me up,
As Hesper, large and brilliant, leads the night!
Our pulses beat together, and our beings
Mixed like two voices in one perfect tune,
And his the richest voice. He loved all things,
From God to foam-bells dancing down a stream,
With a most equal love. Thou mock'st at much;
And he who sneers at any living hope
Or aspiration of a human heart

Is just so many stages less than God,
That universal and all-sided Love.
I'm wretched, Edward! to the very heart;
I see an unreached heaven of young desire
Shine through my hopeless tears. My drooping sails
Flap idly 'gainst the mast of my intent.
I rot upon the waters when my prow
Should grate the golden isles.

EDWARD.

What wouldst thou do?
Thy brain did teem with vapors wild and vast.

WALTER.

But since my younger and my hotter days
(As nebula condenses to an orb),
These vapors gathered to one shining hope,
Sole-hanging in my sky.

EDWARD.

What hope is that?

WALTER.

To set this Age to music, — the great work
Beforé the Poet now. I do believe
When it is fully sung, — its great complaint,
Its hope, its yearning, told to earth and heaven, —

Our troubled age shall pass, as doth a day
That leaves the west all crimson with the promise
Of the diviner morrow, which even then
Is hurrying up the world's great side with light.
Father! if I should live to see that morn,
Let me go upward, like a lark, to sing
One song in the dawning!

EDWARD.

O, you 'd patch with song
The ragged mantle of the beggar earth!
Most hopeless, truly, this of all the tasks
You could put hands to. No, my ardent friend!
You need not tinker at this leaking world;
'T is ruined past all cure.

WALTER.

Edward, for shame!
Not on a path of reprobation runs
The trembling earth. God's eye doth follow her
With far more love than doth her maid, the moon.
Speak no harsh words of Earth; she is our mother,
And few of us, her sons, who have not added
A wrinkle to her brow. She gave us birth,
We drew our nurture from her ample breast,
And there is coming, for us both, an hour
When we shall pray that she will ope her arms

And take us back again. O, I would pledge
My heart, my blood, my brain, to ease the earth
Of but one single pang!

EDWARD.

So would not I.
Because the pangs of earth shall ne'er be eased.
We sleep on velvets now, instead of leaves;
The land is covered with a net of iron,
Upon whose spider-like, far-stretching lines,
The trains are rushing; and the peevish sea
Frets 'gainst the bulging bosoms of the ships
Whose keels have waked it from its hour's repose.
Walter! this height of civilization's tide
Measures our wrong. We 've made the immortal Soul
Slave to the Body. 'T is the Soul has wrought
And laid the iron roads, — evoked a power
Next mightiest to God to drive the trains
That bring the country butter up to town;
Has drawn the terrible lightning from its cloud,
And tamed it to an eager Mercury,
Running with messages of news and grain;
And still the Soul is tasked to harder work,
For Paradise, according to the world,
Is scarce a league a-head.

WALTER.

The man I loved

Wrought this complaint of thine into a song,
Which I sung long ago.

EDWARD.

We must reverse
The plans of ages. Let the Body sweat,
So that the soul be calm, why should *it* work?
Say, had I spent the pith of half my life,
And made me master of our English law,
What gain had I on resurrection morn,
But such as hath the body of a clown,
That it could turn a summerset on earth?
A single soul is richer than all worlds;
Its acts are only shadows of itself,
And oft its wondrous wealth is all unknown;
'T is like a mountain-range, whose rugged sides
Feed starveling flocks of sheep; pierce the bare sides
And they ooze plenteous gold. We must go down
And work our souls like mines, make books our lamps,
Not shrines to worship at, nor heed the world —
Let it go roaring past. You sigh for Fame;
Would serve as long as Jacob for his love,
So you might win her. Spirits calm and still
Are high above your order, as the stars
Sit large and tranquil o'er the restless clouds
That weep and lighten, pelt the earth with hail,
And fret themselves away. The truly great

Rest in the knowledge of their own deserts,
Nor seek the confirmation of the world.
Wouldst thou be calm and still?

WALTER.

I 'd be as lieve
A minnow to leviathan, that draws
A furrow like a ship. Away! away!
You 'd make the world a very oyster-bed.
I 'd rather be the glad, bright-leaping foam,
Than the smooth sluggish sea. O let me live
To love and flush and thrill — or let me die!

EDWARD.

And yet, what weariness was on your tongue
An hour ago! — you shall be wearier yet.

SCENE VII.

A Balcony overlooking the Sea — EDWARD *and* WALTER *seated.*

WALTER.

THE lark is singing in the blinding sky,
Hedges are white with May. The bridegroom sea
Is toying with the shore, his wedded bride,
And, in the fulness of his marriage joy,
He decorates her tawny brow with shells,
Retires a space, to see how fair she looks,
Then proud runs up to kiss her. All is fair —
All glad, from grass to sun! Yet more I love
Than this the shrinking day that sometimes comes
In Winter's front, so fair 'mong its dark peers,
It seems a straggler from the files of June,
Which in its wanderings had lost its wits,
And half its beauty; and, when it returned,
Finding its old companions gone away,

It joined November's troop, then marching past;
And so the frail thing comes, and greets the world
With a thin crazy smile, then bursts in tears,
And all the while it holds within its hand
A few half-withered flowers. I love and pity it!

EDWARD.

Air is like Happiness or Poetry.
We see it in the glorious roof of day,
We feel it lift the down upon the cheek,
We hear it when it sways the heavy woods,
We close our hand on 't — and we have it not.

WALTER.

I 'd be above all things the summer wind
Blowing across a kingdom, rich with alms
From every flower and forest, ruffling oft
The sea to transient wrinkles in the sun,
Where every wrinkle disappears in light.

EDWARD.

Like God, I would pervade Humanity,
From bridegroom dreaming on his marriage morn,
To a wild wretch tied on the farthest bough
Of oak that roars on edge of an abyss,
The while the desperate wind with all its strength

Strains the whole night to drive it down the gulf,
Which like a beast gapes wide for man and tree.
I 'd creep into the lost and ruined hearts
Of sinful women dying in the streets, —
Of pinioned men, their necks upon the block,
Axe gleaming in the air.

WALTER.

Away, away!
Break not, my Edward, this consummate hour;
For very oft within the year that 's past
I 've fought against thy drifts of wintry thought
Till they put out my fires, and I have lain,
A volcano choked with snow. Now let me rest!
If I should wear a rose but once in life,
You surely would not tear it leaf from leaf,
And trample all its sweetness in the dust!
Thy dreary thoughts will make my festal heart
As empty and as desolate 's a church
When worshippers are gone and night comes down.
Spare me this happy hour, and let me rest!

EDWARD.

The banquet you do set before your joys
Is surely but indifferently served,
When they so readily vacate their seats.

WALTER (*abstractedly*).

Would I could raise the dead!
I am as happy as the singing heavens —
There was one very dear to me that died,
With heart as vacant as a last-year's nest.
O, could I bring her back, I 'd empty mine,
And brim hers with my joy! — enough for both.

EDWARD (*after a pause*).

The garrulous sea is talking to the shore,
Let us go down and hear the graybeard's speech.
[*They walk along the sands.*
I shall go down to Bedfordshire to-morrow.
Will you go with me?

WALTER.

Whom shall we see there?

EDWARD.

Why, various specimens of that biped, Man.
I 'll show you one who might have been an abbot
In the old time; a large and portly man,
With merry eyes, and crown that shines like glass.
No thin-smiled April he, bedript with tears,
But appled-Autumn, golden-cheeked and tan;
A jest in his mouth feels sweet as crusted wine.
As if all eager for a merry thought,

The pits of laughter dimple in his cheeks.
His speech is flavorous, evermore he talks
In a warm, brown, autumnal sort of style.
A worthy man, Sir! who shall stand at compt
With conscience white, save some few stains of wine.

WALTER.

Commend me to him! He is half right. The Past
Is but an emptied flask, and the rich Future
A bottle yet uncorked. Who is the next?

EDWARD.

Old Mr. Wilmott, nothing in himself,
But rich as ocean. He has in his hand
Sea-marge and moor, and miles of stream and grove,
Dull flats, scream-startled, as the exulting train
Streams like a meteor through the frighted night,
Wind-billowed plains of wheat, and marshy fens,
Unto whose reeds on midnights blue and cold
Long strings of geese come clanging from the stars.
Yet wealthier in one child than in all these!
O! she is fair as Heaven! and she wears
The sweetest name that woman ever wore,
And eyes to match her name. — 'T is Violet.

WALTER.

If like her name, she must be beautiful.

EDWARD.

And so she is; she has dark violet eyes,
A voice as soft as moonlight. On her cheek
The blushing blood miraculous doth range
From sea-shell pink to sunset. When she speaks
Her soul is shining through her earnest face,
As shines a moon through its up-swathing cloud —
My tongue 's a very beggar in her praise,
It cannot gild her gold with all its words.

WALTER.

Hath unbreeched Cupid struck your heart of ice?
You speak of her as if you were her lover.
Could *you* not find a home within her heart?
No, no! you are too cold, you never loved.

EDWARD.

There 's nothing colder than a desolate hearth.

WALTER.

A desolate hearth! Did fire leap on it once?

EDWARD.

My hand is o'er my heart — and shall remain. —
Let the swift minutes run, red sink the sun,
To-morrow will be rich with Violet.

WALTER.

So be it, large he sinks! Repentant Day
Frees with his dying hand the pallid stars
He held imprisoned since his young hot dawn.
Now watch with what a silent step of fear
They 'll steal out one by one, and overspread
The cool delicious meadows of the night.

EDWARD.

And lo, the first one flutters in the blue
With a quick sense of liberty and joy!
[*Two hours afterwards.*

WALTER.

The rosy glow has faded from the sky,
The rosy glow has faded from the sea.
A tender sadness drops upon my soul
Like the soft twilight dropping on the world.

EDWARD.

Behold yon shining symbol overhead,
Clear Venus hanging in the mellow west,
Jupiter large and sovereign in the east,
With the red Mars between.

WALTER.

See yon poor star

That shudders o'er the mournful hill of pines!
'T would almost make you weep, it seems so sad.
'T is like an orphan trembling with the cold
Over his mother's grave among the pines.
Like a wild lover who has found his love
Worthless and foul, our friend, the sea, has left
His paramour the shore; naked she lies,
Ugly and black and bare. Hark how he moans!
The pain is in his heart. Inconstant fool!
He will be up upon her breast to-morrow
As eager as to-day.

EDWARD.

Like man in that.
We cannot see the lighthouse in the gloom,
We cannot see the rock; but look! now, now,
It opes its ruddy eye, the night recoils,
A crimson line of light runs out to sea,
A guiding torch to the benighted ships.

[*After a long pause*

O God! 'mid our despairs and throbs and pains,
What a calm joy doth fill great Nature's heart!

WALTER.

Thou look'st up to the night as to the face
Of one thou lov'st; I know her beauty is
Deep-mirrored in thy soul as in a sea.

What are thy thinkings of the earth and stars ?—
A theatre magnificently lit
For sorry acting, undeserved applause ?
Dost think there 's any music in the spheres ?
Or doth the whole creation, in thine ear,
Moan like a stricken creature to its God,
Fettered eternal in a lair of pain ?

EDWARD.

I think — we are two fools, let us to bed.
What care the stars for us ?

SCENE VIII.

Evening — A Room in a Manor — Mr. Wilmott, Arthur, Edward, — Walter *seated a little apart.*

WALTER.

She grows on me like moonrise on the night —
My life is shaped in spite of me, the same
As ocean by his shores. Why am I here?
The weary sun was lolling in the west,
Edward and I were sauntering on the shore
Yawning with idleness; and so we came
To kill the tedium of slow-creeping days.
On such slight hinges an existence turns!
How frequent in the very thick of life
We rub clothes with a fate that hurries past!
A tiresome friend detains us in the street,
We part, and, turning, meet fate in the teeth.

A moment more or less had 'voided it.
Yet, through the subtle texture of our souls,
From circumstance each draws a different hue,
As sunlight falling on a bed of flowers,
From the same sunlight one draws crimson deep,
Another azure pale. Edward and I
See Violet each day, her silks brush both.
She smiles on both alike. — My heart! she comes.

[VIOLET *enters and crosses the room.*

O God! I'd be the very floor that bears
Such a majestic thing! Now feed, my eyes,
On beauteous poison, Nightshade, honey sweet.

[*A silence.*

VIOLET.

There is a ghastly chasm in the talk,
As if a fate hung in the midst of us,
It's shadow on each heart. Why, this should be
A dark and lustrous night of wit and wine,
Rich with quick bouts of merry argument,
And witty sallies quenched in laughter sweet,
Yet my voice trembles in a solitude,
Like a lone man in a great wilderness.

MR. WILMOTT.

Arthur, you once could sing a roaring song,
That to the chorus drew our voices out;

'T were no bad plan to sing us one to-night.
Come, wash the roughness from your throat with wine.

ARTHUR.

What sort of song, Sirs, shall I sing to you —
Dame Venus panting on her bed of flowers,
Or Bacchus purple-mouthed astride his tun ?
Now for a headlong song of blooded youth,
Give 't such a welcome as shall lift the roof off —
Sweet friends, be ready with a hip hurra !

ARTHUR *sings.*

A fig for a draught from your crystalline fountains,
        Your cold sunken wells,
        In mid forest dells,
Ha ! bring me the fiery bright dew of the mountains,
When yellowed with peat-reek, and mellowed with age.
        O, richest joy-giver !
        Rare warmer of liver !
Diviner than kisses, thou droll and thou sage !
Fine soul of a land struck with brightest sun-tints,
        Of dark purple moors,
        Of sleek ocean-floors,
Of hills stained with heather like bloody footprints ;
In sunshine, in rain, a flask shall be nigh me,
Warm heart, blood and brain, Fine Sprite deify me !

I've drunk 'mong slain deer in a lone mountain
shieling,
I've drunk till delirious,
While rain beat imperious,
And rang roof and rafter with bagpipes and reeling.
I've drunk in Red Rannoch, amid its gray boulders,
Where, fain to be kissed,
Through his thin scarf of mist
Ben-More to the sun heaves his wet shining shoulders!
I've tumbled in hay with the fresh ruddy lasses,
I've drunk with the reapers,
I've roared with the keepers,
And scared night away with the ring of our glasses!
In sunshine, in rain, a flask shall be nigh me,
Warm heart, blood and brain, Fine Sprite deify me!

Come, string bright songs upon a thread of wine,
And let the coming midnight pass through us,
Like a dusk prince crusted with gold and gems!
Our studious Edward from his Lincoln fens,
And home quaint-gabled hid in rooky trees;
Seen distant is the sun in the arch of noon,
Seen close at hand, the same sun large and red,
His day's work done, within the lazy west
Sitting right portly, staring at the world
With a round, rubicund, wine-bibbing face —

Ha ! like a dove, I see a merry song
Pluming itself for flight upon his lips.

EDWARD *sings.*

My heart is beating with all things that are,
My blood is wild unrest;
With what a passion pants yon eager star
Upon the water's breast!
Clasped in the air's soft arms the world doth sleep,
Asleep its moving seas, its humming lands;
With what an hungry lip the ocean deep
Lappeth forever the white-breasted sands!
What love is in the moon's eternal eyes,
Leaning unto the earth from out the midnight skies!

Thy large dark eyes are wide upon my brow,
Filled with as tender light
As yon low moon doth fill the heavens now,
This mellow autumn night!
On the late flowers I linger at thy feet.
I tremble when I touch thy garment's rim,
I clasp thy waist, I feel thy bosom's beat—
O kiss me into faintness sweet and dim!
Thou leanest to me as a swelling peach,
Full-juiced and mellow, leaneth to the taker's reach.

Thy hair is loosened by that kiss you gave,
  It floods my shoulders o'er;
Another yet! O, as a weary wave
  Subsides upon the shore,
My hungry being with its hopes, its fears,
  My heart like moon-charmed waters, all unrest,
Yet strong as is despair, as weak as tears,
  Doth faint upon thy breast!
I feel thy clasping arms, my cheek is wet
With thy rich tears. One kiss! Sweet, sweet, another
  yet!

I sang this song some twenty years ago
(Hot to the ear-tips, with great thumps of heart),
On the gold lawn, while Cæsar-like the sun
Gathered his robes around him as he fell.

ARTHUR.

Struck by some country cousin, a rosy beauty
Of the Dutch-cheese order, riched with great black eyes
Which, when you planned a theft upon her lips,
Looked your heart quite away!
O Love! O Wine! thou sun and moon o' our lives,
What oysters were we without love and wine!
Our host, I doubt not, vaults a mighty tun,
Wide-wombed and old, cobwebbed and dusted o'er.
Broach! and within its gloomy sides you'll find

A beating heart of wine. The world 's a tun,
A gloomy tun, but he who taps the world
Will find much sweetness in 't. Walter, my boy,
Against this sun of wine's most purple light
Burst into song.

WALTER.

I fear, Sir, I have none.

ARTHUR.

Hang nuts in autumn woods ? Then 't is your trade,
Spin us a new one. Come! some youth love-mad,
Reading the thoughts within his lady's eyes,
Earnest as One that looks into the Book,
Seeking the road to bliss —
Clothe me this bare bough with your sunny flowers.

WALTER.

The evening heaven is not always dressed
With frail cloud-empires of the setting sun,
Nor are we always in our singing-robes.
I have no song, nor can I make you one,
But, with permission, I will tell a tale.

ARTHUR.

If short and merry, Heaven speed your tongue;
If long and sad, the Lord have mercy on us!

WALTER.

Within a city One was born to toil,
Whose heart could not mate with the common doom,
To fall like a spent arrow in the grave.
'Mid the eternal hum, the boy clomb up
Into a shy and solitary youth.
With strange joys and strange sorrows, oft to tears
He was moved, he knew not why, when he has stood
Among the lengthened shadows of the eve,
Such feeling overflowed him from the sky.
Alone he dwelt, solitary as a star
Unsphered and exiled, yet he knew no scorn.
Once did he say, "For me, I'd rather live
With this weak human heart and yearning blood,
Lonely as God, than mate with barren souls;
More brave, more beautiful, than myself must be
The man whom truly I can call my Friend;
He must be an Inspirer, who can draw
To higher heights of Being, and ever stand
O'er me in unreached beauty, like the moon;
Soon as he fail in this, the crest and crown
Of noble friendship, he is naught to me.
What so unguessed as Death? Yet to the dead
It lies as plain as yesterday to us.
Let me go forward to my grave alone;
What need have I to linger by dry wells?"
Books were his chiefest friends. In them he read

Of those great spirits who went down like suns,
And left upon the mountain-tops of Death
A light that made them lovely. His own heart
Made him a Poet. Yesterday to him
Was richer far than fifty years to come.
Alchemist Memory turned his past to gold.
When morn awakes against the dark wet earth,
Back to the morn she laughs with dewy sides,
Up goes her voice of larks! With like effect
Imagination opened on his life,
It lay all lovely in that rarer light.

He was with nature on the Sabbath-days.
Far from the dressed throngs and the city bells,
He gave his hot brows to the kissing wind,
While restless thoughts were stirring in his heart.
" These worldly men will kill me with their scorns,
But Nature never mocks or jeers at me;
Her dewy soothings of the earth and air
Do wean me from the thoughts that mad my brain.
Our interviews are stolen; I can look,
Nature! in thy serene and griefless eyes
But at long intervals; yet, Nature! yet,
Thy silence and the fairness of thy face
Are present with me in the booming streets.
Yon quarry shattered by the bursting fire,
And disembowelled by the biting pick,

Kind Nature! thou hast taken to thyself;
Thy weeping Aprils and soft-blowing Mays,
Thy blossom-buried Junes, have smoothed its scars,
And hid its wounds and trenches deep in flowers.
So take my worn and passion-wasted heart,
Maternal Nature! Take it to thyself,
Efface the scars of scorn, the rents of hate,
The wounds of alien eyes, visit my brain
With thy deep peace, fill with thy calm my heart,
And the quick courses of my human blood."
Thus would he muse and wander till the sun
Reached the red west, where all the waiting clouds,
Attired before in homely dun and gray,
Like Parasites that dress themselves in smiles
To feed a great man's eye, in haste put on
Their purple mantles rimmed with ragged gold,
And congregating in a shining crowd,
Flattered the sinking orb with faces bright.
As slow he journeyed home, the wanderer saw
The laboring fires come out against the dark,
For with the night the country seemed on flame;
Innumerable furnaces and pits,
And gloomy holds, in which that bright slave, Fire,
Doth pant and toil all day and night for man,
Threw large and angry lustres on the sky,
And shifting lights across the long black roads.

Dungeoned in poverty, he saw afar
The shining peaks of fame that wore the sun;
Most heavenly bright, they mocked him through his
bars.
A lost man wildered on the dreary sea,
When loneliness hath somewhat touched his brain,
Doth shrink and shrink beneath the watching sky,
Which hour by hour more plainly doth express
The features of a deadly enemy,
Drinking his woes with a most hungry eye.
Even so, by constant staring on his ills,
They grew worse-featured; till, in his great rage,
His spirit, like a roused sea, white with wrath,
Struck at the stars. "Hold fast! Hold fast! my bra.n!
Had I a curse to kill with, by yon Heaven!
I 'd feast the worms to-night." Dreadfuller words,
Whose very terror blanched his conscious lips,
He uttered in his hour of agony.
With quick and subtle poison in his veins,
With madness burning in his heart and brain,
Wild words, like lightnings, round his pallid lips,
He rushed to die in the very eyes of God.
'T was late, for as he reached the open roads,
Where night was reddened by the drudging fires,
The drowsy steeples tolled the hour of One.
The city now was left long miles behind,
A large black hill was looming 'gainst the stars,

He reached its summit. Far above his head,
Up there upon the still and mighty night,
God's name was writ in worlds. A while he stood,
Silent and throbbing like a midnight star.
He raised his hands; alas! 't was not in prayer —
He long had ceased to pray. "Father," he said,
"I wished to loose some music o'er Thy world,
To strike from its firm seat some hoary wrong,
And then to die in autumn, with the flowers,
And leaves, and sunshine, I have loved so well.
Thou might'st have smoothed my way to some great end —
But wherefore speak? Thou art the mighty God.
This gleaming wilderness of suns and worlds
Is an eternal and triumphant hymn,
Chanted by Thee unto Thine own great self!
Wrapt in thy skies, what were my prayers to Thee?
My pangs? My tears of blood? They could not move
Thee from the depths of Thine immortal dream.
Thou hast forgotten me, God! Here, therefore here,
To-night upon this bleak and cold hill-side,
Like a forsaken watch-fire will I die,
And as my pale corse fronts the glittering night,
It shall reproach Thee before all Thy worlds."
His death did not disturb that ancient Night.
Scornfullest night! Over the dead there hung

Great gulfs of silence, blue, and strewn with stars —
No sound, no motion, in the eternal depths.

EDWARD.

Now, what a sullen-blooded fool was this,
At sulks with earth and Heaven! Could he not
Out-weep his passion like a blustering day,
And be clear-skied thereafter? He, poor wretch,
Must needs be famous! Lord! how Poets geck
At Fame, their idol. Call 't a worthless thing,
Colder than lunar rainbows, changefuller
Than sleeked purples on a pigeon's neck,
More transitory than a woman's loves,
The bubbles of her heart — and yet each mocker
Would gladly sell his soul for one sweet crumb
To roll beneath his tongue.

WALTER.

Alas! the youth,
Earnest as flame, could not so tame his heart
As to live quiet days. When the heart-sick Earth
Turns her broad back upon the gaudy sun,
And stoops her weary forehead to the night,
To struggle with her sorrow all alone,
The moon, that patient sufferer, pale with pain,
Presses her cold lips on her sister's brow,

Till she is calm. But in *his* sorrow's night
He found no comforter. A man can bear
A world's contempt when he has that within
Which says he 's worthy — when he contemns himself,
There burns the hell. So this wild youth was foiled
In a great purpose — in an agony,
In which he learned to hate and scorn himself,
He foamed at God, and died.

MR. WILMOTT.

Rain similes upon his corse like tears —
The youth you spoke of was a glowing moth,
Born in the eve and crushed before the dawn.

VIOLET.

He was, methinks, like that frail flower that comes
Amid the nips and gusts of churlish March,
Drinking pale beauty from sweet April's tears,
Dead on the hem of May.

EDWARD.

A Lapland fool,
Who, staring upward as the Northern Lights
Banner the skies with glory, breaks his heart,
Because his smoky hut and greasy furs
Are not so rich as they.

ARTHUR.

Mine is pathetic —
A ginger-beer bottle burst.

WALTER (*aside*).

And mine would be
The pale child, Eve, leading her mother, Night.

[MR. WILMOTT, ARTHUR, *and* EDWARD, *converse ;*
VIOLET *approaches* WALTER.

VIOLET.

Did you know well that youth of whom you spake ?

WALTER.

Know him ! O, yes, I knew him as myself —
Two passions dwelt at once within his soul,
Like eve and sunset dwelling in one sky.
And as the sunset dies along the west,
Eve higher lifts her front of trembling stars,
Till she is seated in the middle sky,
So gradual, one passion slowly died,
And from its death the other drew fresh life,
Until 't was seated in his soul alone :
The dead was Love — the living, Poetry.

VIOLET.

Alas ! if Love rose never from the dead.

WALTER.

Between him and the lady of his love
There stood a wrinkled worldling ripe for hell.
When with his golden hand he plucked that flower,
And would have smelt it, lo! it paled and shrank,
And withered in his grasp. And when she died,
The rivers of his heart ran all to waste;
They found no ocean, dry sands sucked them up.

Lady! he was a fool — a pitiful fool.
She said she loved him, would be dead in spring—
She asked him but to stand beside her grave —
She said she would be daisies — and she thought
'T would give her joy to feel that he was near.
She died like music; and, would you believe 't?
He kept her foolish words within his heart
As ceremonious as a chapel keeps
A relic of a saint. And in the spring
The doting idiot went!

VIOLET.

What found he there?

WALTER.

Laugh till your sides ache! O, he went, poor fool!
But he found nothing save red trampled clay,
And a dull sobbing rain. Do you not laugh?

Amid the comfortless rain he stood and wept,
Bare-headed in the mocking, pelting rain.
He might have known 't was ever so on earth.

VIOLET.

You cannot laugh yourself, Sir, nor can I.
Her unpolluted corse doth sleep in earth,
Like a pure thought within a sinful soul.
Dearer is earth to God for her sweet sake.

WALTER.

'T is said our nature is corrupt; but she
O'erlaid hers with all graces, even as Night
Wears such a crowd of jewels on her face,
You cannot see 't is black.

VIOLET.

How looked this youth?
Did he in voice or mien resemble you?
Was he about your age? Wore he such curls?
Such eyes of dark sea-blue?

WALTER.

Why do you ask?

VIOLET.

I thought just now you might resemble him.

Were you not brothers ? — twins ? Or was the one
A shadow of the other ?

WALTER.

What mean you ?

VIOLET.

That like the moon you need not wrap yourself
In any cloud ; you shine through each disguise ;
You are a masker in a mask of glass.
You 've such transparent sides, each casual eye
May see the heaving heart.

WALTER.

O, misery !
Is 't visible to thee ?

VIOLET.

'T is clear as dew !
Mine eyes have been upon it all the night,
Unknown to you.

WALTER.

The sorrowful alone
Can know the sorrowful. What woe is thine,
That thou canst read me thus ?

VIOLET.

A new-born power,
Whose unformed features cannot clearly show
Whether 't is Joy or Sorrow. But the years
May nurture it to either.

WALTER.

To thee I 'm bare.
My heart lies open to you, as the earth
To the omniscient sun. I have a work —
The finger of my soul doth point it out;
I trust God's finger points it also out.
I must attempt it; if my sinews fail,
On my unsheltered head men's scorns will fall
Like a slow shower of fire. Yet if one tear
Were mingled with them, it were less to bear.

VIOLET.

I 'll give thee tears —

WALTER.

That were as queenly Night
Would loosen all the jewels from her hair,
And hail them on this sordid thing, the earth.
Thy tears keep for a worthier head than mine.

VIOLET.

I will not cope with you in compliment.

I 'll give you tears, and pity, and true thoughts.
If you are desolate, my heart is open;
I know 't is little worth, but any hut,
However poor, unto a homeless man,
Is welcomer than mists or nipping winds.
But if you conquer Fame ——

WALTER.

With eager hands
I 'll bend the awful thing into a crown,
And you will wear it.

VIOLET.

O, no, no!
Lay it upon *her* grave. [*Another silence.*

ARTHUR.

Run out again!
We should be jovial as the feasting gods.
We 're silent as a synod of the stars!
The night is out at elbows. Laughter 's dead.
To the rescue, Violet! A song! a song!

VIOLET *sings.*

Upon my knee a modern minstrel's tales,
Full as a choir with music, lies unread;
My impatient shallop flaps its silken sails
To rouse me, but I cannot lift my head.

I see a wretched isle, that ghost-like stands
  Wrapt in its mist-shroud in the wintry main;
And now a cheerless gleam of red-ploughed lands,
  O'er which a crow flies heavy in the rain.

I 've neither heart nor voice!

[*Rises and draws the curtain.*

You 've sat the night out, Masters! See, the moon
Lies stranded on the pallid coast of morn.

ARTHUR.

Methinks our merriment lies stranded, too.
Draw the long table for a game of bowls,
You will be captain, Edward, — Gods! he yawns.

[*To* WALTER.

Your thunder, Jove, has soured these cream-pots all.

MR. WILMOTT.

To bed! to bed!

SCENE IX.

A Lawn — Sunset — WALTER *lying at* VIOLET'S *feet.*

VIOLET.

You loved, then, very much this friend of thine ?

WALTER.

The sound of his voice did warm my heart like wine.
He 's long since dead ; but if there is a heaven,
He 's in its heart of bliss.

VIOLET.

How did you live ?

WALTER.

We read and wrote together, slept together ;
We dwelt on slopes against the morning sun,
We dwelt in crowded streets, and loved to walk
While Labor slept ; for, in the ghastly dawn,
The wildered city seemed a demon's brain,

The children of the night its evil thoughts.
Sometimes we sat whole afternoons, and watched
The sunset build a city frail as dream,
With bridges, streets of splendor, towers; and saw
The fabrics crumble into rosy ruins,
And then grow gray as heath. But our chief joy
Was to draw images from everything;
And images lay thick upon our talk,
As shells on ocean sands.

VIOLET.

From everything!
Here is the sunset, yonder grows the moon, —
What image would you draw from these?

WALTER.

Why, this:
The sun is dying like a cloven king
In his own blood; the while the distant moon,
Like a pale prophetess, whom he has wronged,
Leans eager forward, with most hungry eyes,
Watching him bleed to death, and, as he faints,
She brightens and dilates; revenge complete,
She walks in lonely triumph through the night.

VIOLET.

Give not such hateful passion to the orb

That cools the heated lands; that ripes the fields,
While sleep the husbandmen, then hastes away
Ere the first step of dawn, doing all good
In secret and the night. 'T is very wrong.
Would I had known your friend!

WALTER.

Iconoclast!
'T is better as it is.

VIOLET.

Why is it so?

WALTER.

Because you would have loved him, and then I
Would have to wander outside of all joy,
Like Neptune in the cold. [*A pause.*

VIOLET.

Do you remember
You promised yesterday you 'd paint for me
Three pictures from your life?

WALTER.

I 'll do so now.
On this delicious eve, with words like colors,
I 'll limn them on the canvas of your sense.

VIOLET.

Be quick! be quick! for see, the parting sun
But peers above yon range of crimson hills,
Taking his last look of this lovely scene.
Dusk will be here anon.

WALTER.

And all the stars!

VIOLET.

Great friends of yours; you love them overmuch.

WALTER.

I love the stars too much! The tameless sea
Spreads itself out beneath them, smooth as glass.
You cannot love them, lady, till you dwell
In mighty towns; immured in their black hearts,
The stars are nearer to you than the fields.
I 'd grow an Atheist in these towns of trade,
Were 't not for stars. The smoke puts heaven out
I meet sin-bloated faces in the streets,
And shrink as from a blow. I hear wild oaths,
And curses spilt from lips that once were sweet,
And sealed for Heaven by a mother's kiss.
I mix with men whose hearts of human flesh,
Beneath the petrifying touch of gold,
Have grown as stony as the trodden ways.

I see no trace of God, till in the night,
While the vast city lies in dreams of gain,
He doth reveal himself to me in heaven.
My heart swells to Him as the sea to the moon;
Therefore it is I love the midnight stars.

VIOLET.

I would I had a lover who could give
Such ample reasons for his loving me
As you for loving stars! But to your task.

WALTER.

Wilt listen to the pictures from my life?

VIOLET.

Patient as evening to the nightingale!

WALTER.

'Mong the green lanes of Kent — green sunny lanes —
Where troops of children shout, and laugh, and play,
And gather daisies, stood an antique home,
Within its orchard, rich with ruddy fruits;
For the full year was laughing in his prime.
Wealth of all flowers grew in that garden green,
And the old porch with its great oaken door
Was smothered in rose-blooms, while o'er the walls
The honeysuckle clung deliciously.

Before the door there lay a plot of grass,
Snowed o'er with daisies, — flower by all belovèd,
And famousest in song, — and in the midst,
A carvèd fountain stood, dried up and broken,
On which a peacock perched and sunned itself;
Beneath, two petted rabbits, snowy white,
Squatted upon the sward.
A row of poplars darkly rose behind,
Around whose tops, and the old-fashioned vanes,
White pigeons fluttered; and o'er all was bent
The mighty sky, with sailing sunny clouds.
One casement was thrown open, and within
A boy hung o'er a book of poesy,
Silent as planet hanging o'er the sea.
In at the casement open to the noon
Came sweetest garden odors, and the hum —
The drowsy hum — of the rejoicing bees,
Heavened in blooms that overclad the walls;
And the cool wind waved in upon his brow,
And stirred his curls. Soft fell the summer night.
Then he arose, and with inspired lips said, —
" Stars! ye are golden-voicèd clarions
To high-aspiring and heroic dooms.
To-night, as I look up unto ye, Stars!
I feel my soul rise to its destiny,
Like a strong eagle to its eyrie soaring.
Who thinks of weakness underneath ye, Stars?

A hum shall he on earth, a name be heard,
An epitaph shall look up proud to God.
Stars! read and listen, it may not be long."

VIOLET (*leaning over him*).

I'll see that grand desire within your eyes.
O, I only see myself!

WALTER.

Violet!
Could you look through my heart as through mine eyes,
You'd find yourself there, too.

VIOLET.

Hush, flatterer!
Yet go on with your tale.

WALTER.

Three blue days passed,
Full of the sun, loud with a thousand larks;
An evening like a gray child walked 'tween each.
'T was in the quiet of the fourth day's noon,
The boy I speak of slumbered in the wood.
Like a dropt rose at an oak-root he lay,
A lady bent above him. He awoke;
She blushed like sunset, 'mid embarrassed speech;
A shock of laughter made them friends at once,

And laughter fluttered through their after-talk,
As darts a bright bird in and out the leaves.
All day he drank her splendid light of eyes;
Nor did they part until the deepening east
'Gan to be sprinkled with the light of eve.

VIOLET.

Go on! go on!

WALTER.

June sang herself to death.
They parted in the wood, she very pale;
And he walked home the weariest thing on earth.
That night he sat in his unlighted room,
Pale, sad and solitary, sick at heart,
For he had parted with his dearest friends,
High aspirations, bright dreams golden-winged,
Troops of fine fancies that like lambs did play
Amid the sunshine and the virgin dews,
Thick-lying in the green fields of his heart.
Calm thoughts that dwelt like hermits in his soul,
Fair shapes that slept in fancifullest bowers,
Hopes and delights, — he parted with them all.
Linked hand in hand they went, tears in their eyes,
As faint and beautiful as eyes of flowers,
And now he sat alone with empty soul.
Last night his soul was like a forest, haunted

With pagan shapes; when one nymph slumbering lay,
A sweet dream 'neath her eyelids, her white limbs
Sinking full softly in the violets dim;
When timbrelled troops rushed past with branches green.
One in each fountain, riched with golden sands,
With her delicious face a moment seen,
And limbs faint-gleaming through their watery veil.
To-night his soul was like that forest old,
When these were reft away, and the wild wind
Running like one distract 'mong their old haunts,
Gold-sanded fountains, and the bladed flags.

[*A pause.*

It is enough to shake one into tears.
A palace full of music was his heart,
An earthquake rent it open to the rain;
The lovely music died — the bright throngs fled —
Despair came like a foul and grizzly beast,
And littered in its consecrated rooms.

Nature was leaping like a Bacchanal
On the next morn, beneath its sky-wide sheen,
The boy stood pallid in the rosy porch.
The mad larks bathing in the golden light,
The flowers close-fondled by the impassioned winds,
The smells that came and went upon the sense,
Like faint waves on a shore, he heeded not;

He could not look the morning in the eyes.
That singing morn he went forth like a ship;
Long years have passed, and he has not returned,
Beggared or laden, home.

VIOLET.

Ah, me, 't is sad!
And sorrow's hand as well as mine has been
Among these golden curls. 'T is past, 't is past;
It has dissolved, as did the bank of cloud
That lay in the west last night.

WALTER.

I yearned for love,
As earnestly as sun-cracked summer earth
Yearns to the heavens for rain — none ever came.

VIOLET.

O, say not so! I love thee very much;
Let me but grow up like a sweet-breathed flower
Within this ghastly fissure of thy heart!
Do you not love me, Walter?

WALTER.

By thy tears
I love thee as my own immortal soul.
Weep, weep, my Beautiful! Upon thy face

There is no cloud of sorrow or distress;
It is as moonlight, pale, serene and clear.
Thy tears are spilt of joy, they fall like rain
From heaven's stainless blue.
Bend over me, my Beautiful, my Own.
O, I could lie with face upturned forever,
And on thy beauty feed as on a star!

[*Another pause.*

Thy face doth come between me and the heaven —
Start not, my dearest! for I would not give
Thee in thy tears for all yon sky lit up
For a god's feast to-night. And I am loved!
Why did you love me, Violet?

VIOLET.

The sun
Smiles on the earth, and the exuberant earth
Returns the smile in flowers — 't was so with me.
I love thee as a fountain leaps to light —
I can do nothing else.

WALTER.

Say these words again,
And yet again; never fell on my ear
Such drops of music.

VIOLET.

Alas! poor words are weak;

So are the daily ills of common life,
To draw the ingots and the hoarded pearls
From out the treasure-caverns of my heart.
Suffering, despair and death, alone can do it:
Poor Walter! [*Kisses him.*

WALTER.

Gods! I could out-Antony
Antony! This moment I could scatter
Kingdoms like halfpence. I am drunk with joy.
This is a royal hour — the top of life.
Henceforth my path slopes downward to the grave —
All 's dross but love. That largest Son of Time,
Who wandered singing through the listening world,
Will be as much forgot as the canoe
That crossed the bosom of a lonely lake
A thousand years ago. My Beautiful!
I would not give thy cheek for all his songs —
Thy kiss for all his fame. Why do you weep?

VIOLET.

To think that we, so happy now, must die.

WALTER.

That thought hangs like a cold and slimy snail
On the rich rose of love — shake it away —
Give me another kiss, and I will take

Death at a flying leap. The night is fair,
But thou art fairer, Violet! Unloose
The midnight of thy tresses, let them float
Around us both. How the freed ringlets reel
Down to the dewy grass! Here lean thy head,
Now you will feel my heart leap 'gainst thy cheek;
Imprison me with those white arms of thine.
So, so. O sweet upturnéd face! (*Kisses her.*) If God
Told you to-night He 'd grant your dearest wish,
What would it be?

VIOLET.

That He would let you grow
To your ambition's height. What would be yours?

WALTER.

A greater boon than Satan's forfeit throne!
That He would keep us beautiful and young
Forever, as to-night. O, I could live
Unwearied on thy beauty, till the sun
Grows dim and wrinkled as an old man's face.
Our cheeks are close, our breaths mix like our souls.
We have been starved hereto; Love's banquet spread,
Now let us feast our fills.

VIOLET.

Walter!

SCENE X.

A Bridge in a City — Midnight — WALTER *alone.*

WALTER.

ADAM lost Paradise — eternal tale
Repeated in the lives of all his sons.
I had a shining orb of happiness,
God gave it me, but sin passed over it
As small-pox passes o'er a lovely face,
Leaving it hideous. I have lost forever
The Paradise of young and happy thoughts,
And now stand in the middle of my life
Looking back through my tears — ne'er to return.
I 've a stern tryst with Death, and must go on,
Though with slow steps and oft-reverted eyes.

'T is a thick, rich-hazed, sumptuous autumn night;
The moon grows like a white flower in the sky;
The stars are dim. The tired year rests content

Among her sheaves, as a fond mother rests
Among her children ; all her work is done.
There is a weight of peace upon the world ;
It sleeps : God's blessing on it. Not on *me !*
O, as a lewd dream stains the holy sleep,
I stain the holy night, yet dare not die !
I knew this river's childhood, from the lake
That gave it birth, till, as if spilt from heaven,
It floated o'er the face of jet-black rocks,
Graceful and gauzy as a snowy veil.
Then we were pure as the blue sky above us,
Now we are black alike. This stream has turned
The wheels of commerce, and come forth distained
And now trails slowly through a city's heart,
Drawing its filth as doth an evil soul
Attract all evil things ; putrid and black
It mingles with the clear and stainless sea.
So into pure eternity my soul
Will disembogue itself.

Good men have said
That sometimes God leaves sinners to their sin, —
He has left me to mine, and I am changed ;
My worst part is insurgent, and my will
Is weak and powerless as a trembling king
When millions rise up hungry. Woe is me !
My soul breeds sins as a dead body worms !
They swarm and feed upon me. Hear me, God !

Sin met me and enbraced me on my way;
Methought her cheeks were red, her lips had bloom;
I kissed her bold lips, dallied with her hair:
She sang me into slumber. I awoke —
It was a putrid corse that clung to me,
That *clings* to me like memory to the damned,
That rots into my being. Father! God!
I cannot shake it off, it clings, it clings; —
I soon will grow as corrupt as itself. [*A pause.*
God sends me back my prayers, as a father
Returns unoped the letters of a son
Who has dishonored him.
Have mercy, Fiend!
Thou Devil, thou wilt drag me down to hell.
O, if she had proclivity to sin
Who did appear so beauteous and so pure,
Nature may leer behind a gracious mask.
And God himself may be —— I 'm giddy, blind,
The world reels from beneath me.
[*Catches hold of the parapet.*
(*An Outcast approaches.*) Wilt pray for me?

GIRL (*shuddering*).

'T is a dreadful thing to pray.

WALTER.

Why is it so?

Hast thou, like me, a spot upon thy soul
That neither tears can cleanse, nor fires eterne?

GIRL.

But few request *my* prayers.

WALTER.

I request them.
For ne'er did a dishevelled woman cling
So earnest-pale to a stern conqueror's knees,
Pleading for a dear life, as did my prayer
Cling to the knees of God. He shook it off,
And went upon His way. Wilt pray for me?

GIRL.

Sin crusts me o'er as limpets crust the rocks.
I would be thrust from every human door;
I dare not knock at Heaven's.

WALTER.

Poor homeless one!
There is a door stands wide for thee and me —
The door of hell. Methinks we are well met.
I saw a little girl three years ago,
With eyes of azure and with cheeks of red,
A crowd of sunbeams hanging down her face;
Sweet laughter round her; dancing like a breeze.

I 'd rather lair me with a fiend in fire
Than look on such a face as hers to-night.
But I can look on thee, and such as thee;
I 'll call thee "Sister;" do thou call me "Brother."
A thousand years hence, when we both are damned,
We 'll sit like ghosts upon the wailing shore,
And read our lives by the red light of hell.
Will we not, Sister?

GIRL.

O thou strange wild man,
Let me alone: what would you seek with me?

WALTER.

Your ear, my Sister. I have that within
Which urges me to utterance. I could accost
A pensive angel, singing to himself
Upon a hill in heaven, and leave his mind
As dark and turbid as a trampled pool,
To purify at leisure. — I have none
To listen to me, save a sinful woman
Upon a midnight bridge. — She was so fair,
God's eye could rest with pleasure on her face.
O, God, she was so happy! Her short life
As full of music as the crowded June
Of an unfallen orb. What is it now?
She gave me her young heart, full, full of love:

My return — was to break it. Worse, far worse;
I crept into the chambers of her soul,
Like a foul toad, polluting as I went.

GIRL.

I pity her — not you. Man trusts in God;
He is eternal. Woman trusts in man,
And he is shifting sand.

WALTER.

Poor child, poor child!
We sat in dreadful silence with our sin,
Looking each other wildly in the eyes:
Methought I heard the gates of heaven close,
She flung herself against me, burst in tears,
As a wave bursts in spray. She covered me
With her wild sorrow, as an April cloud
With dim dishevelled tresses hides the hill
On which its heart is breaking. She clung to me
With piteous arms, and shook me with her sobs;
For she had lost her world, her heaven, her God,
And now had naught but me and her great wrong.
She did not kill me with a single word,
But once she lifted her tear-dabbled face —
Had hell gaped at my feet I would have leapt
Into its burning throat, from that pale look.
Still it pursues me like a haunting fiend;

It drives me out to the black moors at night,
Where I am smitten by the hissing rain,
And ruffian winds, dislodging from their troops,
Hustle me shrieking, then with sudden turn
Go laughing to their fellows. Merciful God!
It comes — that face again, that white, white face,
Set in a night of hair; reproachful eyes,
That make me mad. O, save me from those eyes!
They will torment me even in the grave,
And burn on me in Tophet.

GIRL.

Where are you going?

WALTER.

My heart's on fire by hell, and on I drive
To outer blackness, like a blazing ship.

[*He rushes away.*

SCENE XI.

Night. — WALTER *standing alone in his garden.*

WALTER.

SUMMER hath murmured with her leafy lips
Around my home, and I have heard her not;
I 've missed the process of three several years,
From shaking wind-flowers to the tarnished gold
That rustles sere on Autumn's aged limbs.
I went three years ago, and now return,
As stag sore-hunted a long summer day
Creeps in the eve to its deep forest-home. [*A pause.*
This is my home again! Once more I hail
The dear old gables and the creaking vanes.
It stands all flecked with shadows in the moon,
Patient, and white and woful. 'T is so still,
It seems to brood upon its youthful years,
When children sported on its ringing floors,
And music trembled through its happy rooms.

'T was here I spent my youth, as far removed
From the great heavings, hopes, and fears of man,
As unknown isle asleep in unknown seas.
Gone my pure heart, and with it happy days;
No manna falls around me from on high,
Barely from off the desert of my life
I gather patience and severe content.
God is a worker. He has thickly strewn
Infinity with grandeur. God is love;
He yet shall wipe away Creation's tears,
And all the worlds shall summer in His smile.
Why work I not? The veriest mote that sports
Its one-day life within the sunny beam
Has its stern duties. Wherefore have I none?
I will throw off this dead and useless past,
As a strong runner, straining for his life,
Unclasps a mantle to the hungry winds.
A mighty purpose rises large and slow
From out the fluctuations of my soul,
As, ghost-like, from the dim and tumbling sea
Starts the completed moon. [*Another pause.*
I have a heart to dare,
And spirit-thews to work my daring out;
I 'll cleave the world as a swimmer cleaves the sea,
Breaking the sleek green billows into froth,
With tilting full-blown chest, and scattering
With scornful breath the kissing, flattering foam,

That leaps and dallies with his dipping lip.
Thou 'rt distant, now, O World! I hear thee not;
There 's no pale fringes of thy fires to-night
Around the large horizon. Yet, O World!
I have thee in my power, and as a man
By some mysterious influence can sway
Another's mind, making him laugh and weep,
Shudder or thrill, such power have I on thee.
Much have I suffered, both from thee and thine;
Thou shalt not 'scape me, World! I 'll make thee weep;
I 'll make my lone thought cross thee like a spirit,
And blanch thy braggart cheeks, lift up thy hair,
And make thy great knees tremble; I will send
Across thy soul dark herds of demon dreams,
And make thee toss and moan in troubled sleep;
And, waking I will fill thy forlorn heart
With pure and happy thoughts, as summer woods
Are full of singing-birds. I come from far,
I 'll rest myself, O World! a while on thee,
And half in earnest, half in jest, I 'll cut
My name upon thee, pass the arch of Death,
Then on a stair of stars go up to God.

SCENE XII.

An Apartment — CHARLES *and* EDWARD *seated.*

EDWARD.

HAVE you seen Walter lately?

CHARLES.

Very much;
I wintered with him.

EDWARD.

What was he about?

CHARLES.

He wrote his Poem then.

EDWARD

That was a hit!
The world is murmuring like a hive of bees;

He is its theme — to-morrow it may change.
Was it done at a dash?

CHARLES.

It was; each word sincere,
As blood-drops from the heart. The full-faced moon,
Set round with stars, in at his casement looked,
And saw him write and write: and when the moon
Was waning dim upon the edge of morn,
Still sat he writing, thoughtful-eyed and pale;
And, as of yore, round his white temples reeled
His golden hair, in ringlets beautiful.
Great joy he had, for thought came glad and thick
As leaves upon a tree in primrose-time;
And as he wrote his task the lovelier grew,
Like April unto May, or as a child,
A-smile in the lap of life, by fine degrees
Orbs to a maiden, walking with meek eyes
In atmosphere of beauty round her breathed.
He wrote all winter in an olden room,
Hallowed with glooms and books. Priests who have wed
Their makers unto Fame, Moons that have shed
Eternal halos around England's head;
Books dusky and thumbed without, *within*, a sphere
Smelling of Spring, as genial, fresh, and clear,
And beautiful as is the rainbowed air

After May showers. Within this pleasant lair
He passed in writing all the winter moons;
But when May came, with train of sunny noons,
He chose a leafy summer-house within
The greenest nook in all his garden green;
Oft a fine thought would flush his face divine,
As he had quaffed a cup of olden wine,
Which deifies the drinker: oft his face
Gleamed like a spirit's in that shady place,
While he saw, smiling upward from the scroll,
The image of the thought within his soul;
There, 'mid the waving shadows of the trees,
'Mong garden-odors and the hum of bees,
He wrote the last and closing passages.
He is not happy.

EDWARD.

Has he told you so?

CHARLES.

Not in plain terms. Oft an unhappy thought,
Telling all is not well, falls from his soul
Like a diseaséd feather from the wing
Of a sick eagle; a scorched meteor-stone
Dropt from the ruined moon.

EDWARD.

What are these thoughts?

CHARLES.

I walked with him upon a windy night;
We saw the streaming moon flee through the sky
Pursued by all the dark and hungry clouds.
He stopped and said: "Weariness feeds on all.
That vampire, Time, shall yet suck dim the sun.
God wearies, and so makes a universe,
And gathers angels round Him. — He is weak;
I weary, and so wreak myself in verse.
Which but relieves me as a six-inch pipe
Relieves the dropsied sea. O, for mad War!
I'd give my next twelve years to head but once
Ten thousand horse in a victorious charge.
Give me some one to hate, and let me chase
Him through the zones, and finding him at last,
Make his accursed eyes leap on his cheeks,
And his face blacken, with one choking gripe."

EDWARD.

Savage enough, i' faith!

CHARLES.

He often said,

His strivings after Poesy and Fame
Were vain as turning blind eyes on the sun.
His Book came out; I told him that the world
Hailed him a poet. He said, with feeble smile,
"I have arisen like a dawn — the world,
Like the touched Memnon, murmurs — that is all."
He said, as we were lying on the moss
(A forest sounding o'er us, like a sea
Above two mermen seated on the sands),
"Our human hearts are deeper than our souls,
And Love than Knowledge is diviner food —
O, Charles! if God will ever send to thee
A heart that loves thee, reverence that heart.
We think that Death is hard, when he can kill
An infant smiling in his very face:
Harder was I than Death. — In cup of sin
I did dissolve thee, thou most precious pearl,
Then drank thee up." We sat one eve,
Gazing in silence on the falling sun:
We saw him sink. Upon the silent world,
Like a fine veil, came down the tender gloom;
A dove came fluttering round the window, flew
Away, and then came fluttering back. He said,
"As that dove flutters round the casement, comes
A pale shape round my soul; I 've done it wrong,
I never will be happy till I ope

My heart and take it in." — 'T was ever so;
To some strange sorrow all his thoughts did tend,
Like waves unto a shore. Dost know his grief?

EDWARD.

I dimly guess it; a rich cheek grew pale,
A happy spirit singing on her way
Grew mute as winter. Walter, mad and blind,
Threw off the world, God, unclasped pleading arms,
Rushed wild through Pleasure and through Devil-world,
Till he fell down exhausted. — Do you know
If he believes in God?

CHARLES.

He told me once,
The saddest thing that can befall a soul
Is when it loses faith in God and Woman;
For he had lost them both. — Lost I those gems —
Though the world's throne stood empty in my path,
I would go wandering back into my childhood,
Searching for them with tears.

EDWARD.

Let him go
Alone upon his waste and dreary road.
He will return to the old faith he learned

Beside his mother's knee. That memory
That haunts him, as the sweet and gracious moon
Haunts the poor outcast Earth, will lead him back
To happiness and God.

CHARLES.

May it be so!

SCENE XIII.

Afternoon. — WALTER *and* VIOLET *entering the garden from the house.*

VIOLET.

THIS is the dwelling you have told me of, —
Summer again hath dressed its bloomy walls,
Its fragrant front is populous with bees;
This is the garden — all is very like,
And yet unlike the picture in my heart;
I know not which is loveliest. I see
Afar the wandering beauty of the stream,
And nearer I can trace it as it shows
Its broad and gleaming back among the woods.
Is that the wood you slept in?

WALTER.

That is it,

And every nook and glade and tangled dell,
From its wide circle to its leafy heart,
Is as familiar to me as my soul.
Memories dwell like doves among the trees,
Like nymphs in glooms, like naïads in the wells;
And some are sweet, and sadder some than death.

[*A pause.*

I could have sworn the world did sing in air,
I was so happy once. The eagle drinks
The keen blue morning, and the morn was mine.
I bathed in sunset, and to me the night
Was a perpetual wonder and an awe.
Oft, as I lay on earth and gazed at her,
The gliding moon with influence divine
Would draw a most delicious tide of tears
And spill it o'er my eyes. (Sadness was joy
Of but another sort.) My happiness
Was flecked with vague and transitory griefs,
As sweetly as the shining length of June
With evanescent eves; and through my soul
At intervals a regal pageant passed,
As through the palpitating streets the corse
Of a great chieftain, rolled in music rich,
Moves slowly towards its rest. In these young days
Existence was to me sufficient joy;
At once a throne and kingdom, crown and lyre.
Now it is but a strip of barren sand,

On which with earnest heart I strive to rear
A temple to the gods. I will not sadden you.
[*They move on.*
This is the fountain: once it flashed and sang
(Possessed of such exuberance of joy)
To golden sunrise, the blue day, and when
The night grew gradual o'er it, star by star,—
Now it is mute as Memnon.

VIOLET.

Sad again!
Its brim is written over — o'er and o'er;
'T is mute; but have you made its marble lips
As sweet as Music's?

WALTER.

Miserable words!
The offspring of some most unhappy hours.
To me this fountain's brim is sad as though
'T were splashed with my own blood.

VIOLET (*reads*).

"Nature cares not
Although her loveliness should ne'er be seen
By human eyes, nor praised by human tongues.
The cataract exults among the hills,
And wears its crown of rainbows all alone.

Libel the ocean on his tawny sands,
Write verses in his praise, — the unmoved sea
Erases both alike. Alas for man!
Unless his fellows can behold his deeds
He cares not to be great." 'T is very true.
The next is written in a languid hand:
" Sin has drunk up my pleasure, as eclipse
Drinks up the sunlight. On my spirit lies
A malison and ban. What though the Spring
Makes all the hills and valleys laugh in green, —
Is the sea healed, or is the plover's cry
Merry upon the moor? I now am kin
To these, and winds, and ever-suffering things."
O, I could blot these words out with my tears!

WALTER.

So could I when I wrote them.

VIOLET.

What is the next?
" A sin lies dead and dreadful in my soul,
Why should I gaze upon it day by day?
O, rather, since it cannot be destroyed,
Let me as reverently cover it
As with a cloak we cover up the dead,
And place it in some chamber of my soul,

Where it may lie unseen as sound, yet *felt*, —
Making life hushed and awful."

WALTER.

No more. No more.
Let God wash out this record with His rain!
This is the summer-house. [*They enter.*
It is as sweet
As if enamored Summer did adorn
It for his Love to dwell in. I love to sit
And hear the pattering footsteps of the shower,
As he runs over it, or watch at noon
The curious sunbeams peeping through the leaves.

VIOLET.

I 've always pictured you in such a place
Writing your Book, and hurrying on, as if
You had a long and wondrous tale to tell,
And felt Death's cold hand closing round your heart.

WALTER.

Have you read my book?

VIOLET.

I have.

WALTER.

It is enough.
The Book was only written for two souls,
And they are thine and mine.

VIOLET.

For many weeks,
When I was dwelling by the moaning sea,
Your name was blown to me on every wind,
And I was glad; for by that sign I knew
You had fulfilled your heart, and hoped you would
Put off the robes of sorrow, and put on
The singing crown of Fame. One dreary morn
Your Book came to me, and I fondled it,
As though it were a pigeon sent from thee
With love beneath its wing. I read and read
Until the sun lifted his cloudy lids
And shot wild light along the leaping deep,
Then closed his eyes in death. I shed no tear.
I laid it down in silence, and went forth
Burdened with its sad thoughts: slowly I went;
And, as I wandered through the deepening gloom,
I saw the pale and penitential moon
Rise from dark waves that plucked at her, and go
Sorrowful up the sky. Then gushed my tears —
The tangled problem of my life was plain —
I cried aloud, "O, would he come to me!

I know he is unhappy; that he strives
As fiercely as that blind and desperate sea,
Clutching with all his waves — in vain, in vain.
He never will be happy till he comes."
As I went home the thought that you would come
Filled my lorn heart with gladness, as the moon
Filled the great vacant night with moonlight, till
Its silver bliss ran o'er — so after prayer
I slept in the lap of peace — next morn you came.

WALTER.

And then I found you beautiful and pale —
Pale as that moonlight night! O Violet,
I have been undeceived. In my hot youth
I kissed the painted bloom off Pleasure's lips
And found them pale as Pain's, — and wept aloud.
Never henceforward can I hope to drain
The rapture of a lifetime at a gulp.
My happiness is not a troubled joy;
'T is deep, serene as death. The sweet contents,
The happy thoughts from which I've been estranged,
Again come round me, as the old known peers
Surround and welcome a repentant spirit,
Who by the steps of sorrow hath regained
His throne and golden prime. The eve draws nigh!
The prosperous sun is in the west, and sees
From the pale east to where he sets in bliss,

His long road glorious. Wilt thou sing, my love,
And sadden me into a deeper joy?

VIOLET *sings.*

The wondrous ages pass like rushing waves,
Each crowned with its own foam. Bards die, and
Fame
Hangs like a pallid meteor o'er their graves.
Religions change, and come and go like flame.

Nothing remains but Love: the world's round mass
It doth pervade, all forms of life it shares,
The institutions that like moments pass
Are but the shapes the masking spirit wears.
Love is a sanctifier; 't is a moon,
Turning each dusk to silver. A pure light,
Redeemer of all errors ——

[*Ceases, and bursts into tears.*

WALTER.

What ails you, Violet?
Has music stung you like a very snake?
Why do you weep?

VIOLET.

Walter! dost thou believe
Love will redeem all errors? O, my friend,

This gospel saves you! doubt it, you are lost.
Deep in the mists of sorrow long I lay,
Hopeless and still, when suddenly *this* truth
Like a slant sunbeam quivered through the mist,
And turned it into radiance. In the light
I wrote these words, while you were far away
Fighting with shadows. O! Walter, in one boat
We floated o'er the smooth, moon-silvered sea;
The sky was smiling with its orbs of bliss;
And while we lived within each other's eyes,
We struck and split, and all the world was lost
In one wild whirl of horror darkening down;
At last I gained a deep and silent isle,
Moaned on by a dim sea, and wandered round
Week after week the happy-mournful shore,
Wondering if you had 'scaped.

WALTER.

Thou noble soul,
Teach me, if thou art nearer God than I!
My life was a long dream; when I awoke,
Duty stood like an angel in my path,
And seemed so terrible, I could have turned
Into my yesterdays, and wandered back
To distant childhood, and gone out to God
By the gate of birth, not death. Lift, lift me up
By thy sweet inspiration, as the tide

Lifts up a stranded boat upon the beach.
I will go forth 'mong men, not mailed in scorn,
But in the armor of a pure intent.
Great duties are before me and great songs,
And whether crowned or crownless when I fall,
It matters not, so as God's work is done.
I 've learned to prize the quiet lightning-deed,
Not the applauding thunder at its heels
Which men call Fame. Our night is past;
We stand in precious sunrise, and beyond
A long day stretches to the very end.
Look out, my beautiful, upon the sky!
Even puts on her jewels. Look! she sets,
Venus upon her brow. (I never gaze
Upon the evening but a tide of awe,
And love, and wonder, from the Infinite,
Swells up within me, as the running brine
From the smooth-glistening, wide-heaving sea,
Grows in the creeks and channels of a stream
Until it threats its banks. It is not joy,
'T is sadness more divine.)

VIOLET.

How quick they come, —
World after world! See the great moon above
Yon undistinguishable clump of trees
Is slowly from the darkness gathering light!
You used to love the moon!

WALTER.

This mournful wind
Has surely been with Winter, 't is so cold.
The dews are falling, Violet! Your cloak —
Draw it around you. Let the still night shine!
A star 's a cold thing to a human heart,
And love is better than their radiance. Come!
Let us go in together.

AN EVENING AT HOME.

To-day a chief was buried — let him rest.
His country's bards are up like larks, and fill
With singing the wide heavens of his fame.
To-night I sit within my lonely room,
The atmosphere is full of misty rain,
Wretched the earth and heaven. Yesterday
The streets and squares were choked with yellow fogs.
To-morrow we may all be drenched in sleet!
Stretched like a homeless beggar on the ground,
The city sleeps amid the misty rain.
Though Rain hath pitched his tent above my head,
'T is but a speck upon the happy world.
Since I 've began to trace these lines, Sunrise
Has struck a land and woke its bleating hills;
Afar upon some black and silent moor
The crystal stars are shaking in the wind;
An ocean gurgles, for the stooping moon

Hath kissed him into peace, and now she smooths
The well-pleased monster with her silver hand.
Come, naked, gleaming Spring! great crowds of larks
Fluttering above thy head, thy happy ears
Loud with their ringing songs, Bright Saviour, come!
And kill old Winter with thy glorious look,
And turn his corse to flowers!

I sit to-night
As dreary as the pale, deserted East,
That sees the Sun, the Sun that once was hers,
Forgetful of her, flattering his new love,
The happy-blushing West. In these long streets
Of traffic and of noise, the human hearts
Are hard and loveless as a wreck-strewn coast.
Eternity doth wear upon her face
The veil of Time. They only see the veil,
And thus they know not what they stand so near.
O, rich in gold! Beggars in heart and soul!
Poor as the empty void! Why, even I,
Sitting in this bare chamber with my thoughts,
Am richer than ye all, despite your bales,
Your streets of warehouses, your mighty mills,
Each booming like a world faint heard in space;
Your ships; unwilling fires, that day and night
Writhe in your service seven years, then die
Without one taste of peace. Do ye believe

A simple primrose on a grassy bank
Forth-peeping to the sun, a wild bird's nest,
The great orb dying in a ring of clouds, —
Like hoary Jacob 'mong his waiting sons, —
The rising moon, and the young stars of God,
Are things to love! With *these* my soul is brimmed;
With a diviner and serener joy
Than all thy heaven of money-bags can bring
Thy dry heart, Worldling!

The terror-stricken rain
Flings itself wildly on the window-panes,
Imploring shelter from the chasing wind.
Alas! to-night in this wide waste of streets
It beats on human limbs as well as walls!
God led Eve forth into the empty world
From Paradise. Could our great Mother come
And see her children now, what sight were worst,
A worker woke by cruel Day, the while
A kind dream feeds with sweetest phantom-bread
Him and his famished ones; or, when the Wind,
With shuddering fingers, draws the veil of smoke,
And scares her with a battle's bleeding face?

Most brilliant star upon the crest of Time
Is England. England! O, I know a tale
Of those far summers when she lay in the sun,

Listening to her own larks, with growing limbs,
And mighty hands, which since have tamed the world,
Dreaming about their tasks. This dreary night
I 'll tell the story to my listening heart.
I sang 't to thee, O unforgotten Friend!
(Who dwellest now on breezy English downs,
While I am drowning in the hateful smoke)
Beside the river which I long have loved.
O happy Days! O happy, happy Past!
O Friend! I am a lone benighted ship;
Before me hangs the vast untravelled gloom,
Behind a wake of splendor fading fast
Into the hungry gloom from whence it came.

Two days the Lady gazed toward the west,
The way that he had gone; and when the third
From its high noon sloped to a rosy close,
Upon the western margin of the isle,
Feeding her petted swans by tossing bread
Among the clumps of water-lilies white,
She stood. The fond Day pressed against her face;
His amorous, airy fingers with her robe
Fluttered and played, and trembling touched her throat,
And toying with her ringlets could have died
Upon her sweet lips and her happy cheeks!
With a long rippling sigh she turned away,
And wished the sun was underneath the hills.

Anon she sang, and ignorant Solitude,
Astonished at the marvel of her voice,
Stood tranced and mute as savage at the door
Of rich cathedral when the organ rolls,
And all the answering choirs awake at once.
Then she sat down and thought upon her love;
Fed on the various wonders of his face,
To make his absence rich. "'T is but three days
Since he went from me in his light canoe,
And all the world went with him; and to-night
He will be back again. O, when he comes,
And when my head is laid upon his breast,
And in the pauses of the sweetest storm
Of kisses that e'er beat upon a face,
I 'll tell him how I 've pined, and sighed, and wept,
And thought of those sweet days and nights that flew
O'er us unheeded as a string of swans,
That wavers down the sky toward the sea, —
And he will chide me into blissful tears,
Then kiss the tears away." Quick leapt she up.
"He comes! he comes!" She laughed and clapt her hands.
A light canoe came dancing o'er the lake,
And he within it gave a cry of joy.
She sent an answer back that drew him on.
The swans are scared, — the lilies rippled, — now
Her happy face is hidden in his breast,

And words are lost in joy. "My Bertha! let
Me see myself again in those dear orbs.
Have you been lonely, love?" She raised her head.
"You surely will not leave me so again!
I'll grow as pale 's the moon, and my praised cheeks
Will be as wet as April's, if you do."
As, when the moon hath sleeked the blissful sea,
A light wind wrinkles it and passes off,
So ran a transient trouble o'er his face.
"My Bertha! we must leave this isle to-night.
Thy shining face is blanked! We will return
Ere thrice the day, like a great bird of light
Flees 'cross the dark, and hides it with its wings."
"Ah, wherefore?" "Listen, I will tell you why.

"I stood afar upon the grassy hills.
I saw the country, with its golden slopes,
And woods, and streams, run down to meet the sea.
I saw the basking ocean skinned with light.
I saw the surf upon the distant sands
Silent and white as snow. Above my head
A lark was singing, 'neath a sunny cloud,
Around the playing winds. As I went down
There seemed a special wonder on the shore,
Low murmuring crowds around a temple stood:
There was a wildered music on the air,
Which came and went, yet ever nearer grew,

When, lo! a train came upward from the sea
With snowy garments, and with reverend steps.
Full in their front a silver cross they bore,
And this sweet hymn they strewed along the winds.

'Blest be this sunny morning, sweet and fair!
Blest be the people of this pleasant land!
Ye unseen larks that sing a mile in air,
Ye waving forests, waving green and grand,
Ye waves, that dance upon the flashing strand,
Ye children golden-haired! we bring, we bring
A gospel hallowing.'
Then one stood forth and spoke against the gods;
He called them 'cruel gods,' and then he said,
'We have a Father, One who dwells serene,
'Bove thunder and the stars, whose eye is mild,
And ever open as the summer sky;
Who cares for everything on earth alike,
Who hears the plovers crying in the wind,
The happy linnets singing in the broom,
Whose smile is sunshine.' When the old man ceased,
Forth from the murmuring crowd there stepped a youth
As bright-haired as a star, and cried aloud,
'Friends! I've grown up among the wilds, and found
Each outward form is but a window whence
Terror or Beauty looks. Beauty I've seen
In the sweet eyes of flowers, along the streams,

And in the cold and crystal wells that sleep
Far in the murmur of the summer woods;
Terror in fire and thunder, in the worn
And haggard faces of the winter clouds,
In shuddering winds, and oft on moonless nights
I 've heard it in the white and wailing fringe
That runs along the coast from end to end.
The mountains brooded on some wondrous thought
Which they would ne'er reveal. I seemed to stand
Outside of all things; my desire to know
Grew wild and eager as a starving wolf.
To gain the secret of the awful world,
I knelt before the gods, and then held up
My heart to them in the pure arms of prayer, —
They gave no answer, or had none to give.
Friends! I will test these sour and sullen gods:
If they are weak, 't is well, we then may list
Unto the strangers; but if my affront
Draw angry fire, I shall be slain by gods,
And Death may have no secrets. A spear! a steed!'
A steed was brought by trembling hands, he sprang
And dashed towards the temple with a cry.
A shudder ran through all the pallid crowds.
I saw him enter, and my sight grew dim,
And on a long-suspended breath I stood,
Till one might count a hundred beats of heart:
Then he rode slowly forth, and, wondrous strange!

Although an awful gleam lay on his face,
His charger's limbs were drenched with terror-sweat.
Amid the anxious silence loud he cried,
'Gods, marvellously meek! Why, any child
May pluck them by the beard, spit in their face,
Or smite them on the mouth; they can do naught
But sit like poor old foolish men, and moan.
I flung my spear.'—Here, as a singing rill
Is in the mighty noise of ocean drowned,
His voice was swallowed in the shout that rose,
And touched the heavens, ran along the hills,
Thence came on after-silence, strange and dim.

A voice rose 'mong the strangers, like a lark,
And warbled out its joy, then died away.
And the old man that spoke before went on,
And, O! the gentle music of his voice
Stirred through my heart-strings like a wind through reeds.
He said, 'It was God's hand that shaped the world
And laid it in the sunbeams:' and that 'God
With His great presence fills the universe.
That could we dwell like night among the stars,
Or plunge with whales in the unsounded sea,
He still would be around us with His care.'
And also, That as flowers come back in Spring,

We would live after Death.' I heard no more.
I thought of thee in this delightful isle,
Pure as a prayer, and wished that I had wings
To tell you swiftly that the death we feared
Was but a gray eve 'tween two shining days,
That we would love forever! Then I thought
Our home might be in that transparent star
Which we have often watched from off this verge
Stand in the dying sunset large and clear.
The humming world awoke me from my dream.
I saw the old gods tumbled on the grass
Like uncouth stones, they threw the temple wide,
And Summer, with her bright and happy face,
Looked in upon its gloom, and pensive grew.
The while among the tumult of the crowds
Divinest hymns the white-robed strangers sang.
I wearied for thee, Bertha! and I came.
Wilt go and hear these strangers?" She turned on him
A look of love — a look that richly crowned
A moment heavenly rich, and murmured "Yes."
He kissed her proudly, while a giddy tear,
Wild with its happiness, ran down her cheek
And perished in the dew. They took their seats,
And as the paddles struck, gray-pinioned Time
Flew through the gates of sunset into Night,
And held through stars to gain the coasts of Morn.

'T is done! The phantoms of my soul have fled
Into the night, and I am left alone
With that sweet sadness which doth ever dwell
On the brink of tears; I stare i' the crumbling fire,
Which from my brooding eye takes strangest shapes.
The Past is with me, and I scarcely hear
Outside the weeping of the homeless rain.

LADY BARBARA.

EARL GAWAIN wooed the Lady Barbara,—
High-thoughted Barbara, so white and cold!
'Mong broad-branched beeches in the summer shaw,
In soft green light his passion he has told.
When rain-beat winds did shriek across the wold,
The Earl to take her fair reluctant ear
Framed passion-trembled ditties manifold;
Silent she sat his amorous breath to hear,
With calm and steady eyes, her heart was otherwhere

He sighed for her through all the summer weeks;
Sitting beneath a tree whose fruitful boughs
Bore glorious apples with smooth-shining cheeks,
Earl Gawain came and whispered, "Lady, rouse!
Thou art no vestal held in holy vows,
Out with our falcons to the pleasant heath."
Her father's blood leapt up unto her brows—

He who, exulting on the trumpet's breath,
Came charging like a star across the lists of death.

Trembled, and passed before her high rebuke:
And then she sat, her hands clasped round her knee·
Like one far-thoughted was the lady's look,
For in a morning cold as misery
She saw a lone ship sailing on the sea;
Before the north 't was driven like a cloud,
High on the poop a man sat mournfully:
The wind was whistling thorough mast and shroud,
And to the whistling wind thus did he sing aloud:

"Didst look last night upon my native vales,
Thou Sun, that from the drenching sea hast clomb?
Ye demon winds, that glut my gaping sails,
Upon the salt sea must I ever roam,
Wander forever on the barren foam?
O happy are ye, resting mariners!
O Death, that thou wouldst come and take me home!
A hand unseen this vessel onward steers,
And onward I must float through slow moon-measured
years.

"Ye winds! when like a curse ye drove us on,
Frothing the waters, and along our way,
Nor cape, nor headland, through red mornings shone,

One wept aloud, one shuddered down to pray,
One howled, 'Upon the deep we are astray.'
On our wild hearts his words fell like a blight:
In one short hour my hair was stricken gray,
For all the crew sank ghastly in my sight
As we went driving on through the cold starry night.

"Madness fell on me in my loneliness,
The sea foamed curses, and the reeling sky
Became a dreadful face which did oppress
Me with the weight of its unwinking eye.
It fled, when I burst forth into a cry —
A shoal of fiends came on me from the deep,
I hid, but in all corners they did pry,
And dragged me forth, and round did dance and leap;
They mouthed on me in dream, and tore me from sweet sleep.

"Strange constellations burned above my head,
Strange birds around the vessel shrieked and flew,
Strange shapes, like shadows, through the clear sea fled,
As our lone ship, wide-winged, came rippling through,
Angering to foam the smooth and sleeping blue."
The lady sighed, "Far, far upon the sea,
My own Sir Arthur, could I die with you!
The wind blows shrill between my love and me."
Fond heart! the space between was but the apple-tree.

There was a cry of joy; with seeking hands
She fled to him, like worn bird to her nest;
Like washing water on the figured sands,
His being came and went in sweet unrest,
As from the mighty shelter of his breast
The Lady Barbara her head uprears
With a wan smile, "Methinks I 'm but half blest;
Now when I 've found thee, after weary years,
I cannot see thee, love! so blind I am with tears."

TO——.

THE broken moon lay in the autumn sky,
  And I lay at thy feet;
You bent above me; in the silence I
  Could hear my wild heart beat.

I spoke; my soul was full of trembling fears
  At what my words would bring:
You raised your face, your eyes were full of tears,
  As the sweet eyes of Spring.

You kissed me then, I worshipped at thy feet
  Upon the shadowy sod.
O, fool, I loved thee! loved thee, lovely cheat!
  Better than Fame or God.

My soul leaped up beneath thy timid kiss:
What then to me were groans,
Or pain, or death? Earth was a round of bliss,
I seemed to walk on thrones.

And you were with me 'mong the rushing wheels,
'Mid Trade's tumultuous jars;
And where to awe-struck wilds the Night reveals
Her hollow gulfs of stars.

Before your window, as before a shrine,
I 've knelt 'mong dew-soaked flowers,
While distant music-bells, with voices fine,
Measured the midnight hours.

There came a fearful moment: I was pale,
You wept, and never spoke,
But clung around me as the woodbine frail
Clings, pleading, round an oak.

Upon my wrong I steadied up my soul,
And flung thee from myself;
I spurned thy love as 't were a rich man's dole, —
It was my only wealth.

I spurned thee! I, who loved thee, could have died,
That hoped to call thee "wife,"
And bear thee, gently smiling at my side,
Through all the shocks of life!

Too late, thy fatal beauty and thy tears,
Thy vows, thy passionate breath;
I 'll meet thee not in Life, nor in the spheres
Made visible by Death.

SONNETS.

I CANNOT deem why men toil so for Fame.
A porter is a porter though his load
Be the oceaned world, and although his road
Be down the ages. What is in a name?
Ah! 't is our spirit's curse to strive and seek.
Although its heart is rich in pearls and ores,
The sea complains upon a thousand shores;
Sea-like we moan forever. We are weak.
We ever hunger for diviner stores.
I cannot say I have a thirsting deep
For human fame, nor is my spirit bowed
To be a mummy above ground to keep
For stare and handling of the vulgar crowd,
Defrauded of my natural rest and sleep.

THERE have been vast displays of critic wit
O'er those who vainly flutter feeble wings,
Nor rise an inch 'bove ground, — weak Poetlings!
And on them to the death men's brows are knit.
Ye men! ye critics! seems 't so very fit
They on a storm of laughter should be blown
O'er the world's edge to Limbo? Be it known,
Ye men! ye critics! that beneath the sun
The chiefest woe is this, — When all alone,
And strong as life, a soul's great currents run
Poesy-ward, like rivers to the sea,
But never reach 't. Critic, let that soul moan
In its own hell without a kick from thee.
Kind Death, kiss gently, ease this weary one!

Joy like a stream flows through the Christmas-streets,
But I am sitting in my silent room,
Sitting all silent in congenial gloom.
To-night, while half the world the other greets
With smiles and grasping hands and drinks and meats,
I sit and muse on my poetic doom;
Like the dim scent within a budded rose,
A joy is folded in my heart; and when
I think on Poets nurtured 'mong the throes,
And by the lowly hearths of common men, —
Think of their works, some song, some swelling ode
With gorgeous music growing to a close,
Deep-muffled as the dead-march of a god, —
My heart is burning to be one of those.

Beauty still walketh on the earth and air;
Our present sunsets are as rich in gold
As ere the Iliad's music was out-rolled;
The roses of the Spring are ever fair,
'Mong branches green still ring-doves coo and pair
And the deep sea still foams its music old.
So, if we are at all divinely souled,
This beauty will unloose our bonds of care.
'T is pleasant, when blue skies are o'er us bending
Within old starry-gated Poesy,
To meet a soul set to no worldly tune,
Like thine, sweet Friend! O, dearer this to me
Than are the dewy trees, the sun, the moon,
Or noble music with a golden ending.

LAST night my cheek was wetted with warm tears,
Each worth a world. They fell from eyes divine.
Last night a loving lip was pressed to mine,
And at its touch fled all the barren years;
And softly couched upon a bosom white,
Which came and went beneath me like a sea,
An emperor I lay in empire bright,
Lord of the beating heart, while tenderly
Love-words were glutting my love-greedy ears.
Kind Love, I thank thee for that happy night!
Richer this cheek with those warm tears of thine
Than the vast midnight with its gleaming spheres.
Leander toiling through the midnight brine,
Kingdomless Antony, were scarce my peers.

I WROTE a Name upon the river sands,
With her who bore it standing by my side,
Her large dark eyes lit up with gentle pride,
And leaning on my arm with claspéd hands.
To burning words of mine she thus replied:
"Nay, writ not on thy heart. This tablet frail
Fitteth as frail a vow. Fantastic bands
Will scarce confine these limbs." I turned love-pale,
I gazed upon the rivered landscape wide,
And thought how little *it* would all avail
Without her love. 'T was on a morn of May;
Within a month I stood upon the sand,
Gone was the name I traced with trembling hand,—
And from my heart 't was also gone away.

LIKE clouds or streams we wandered on at will,
Three glorious days, till, near our journey's end,
As down the moorland road we straight did wend,
To Wordsworth's "Inversneyd," talking to kill
The cold and cheerless drizzle in the air,
'Bove me I saw, at pointing of my friend,
An old Fort like a ghost upon the hill,
Stare in blank misery through the blinding rain;
So human-like it seemed in its despair —
So stunned with grief — long gazed at it we twain.
Weary and damp we reached our poor abode;
I, warmly seated in the chimney-nook,
Still saw that old Fort o'er the moorland road
Stare through the rain with strange woe-wildered look.

SHEATHED is the river as it glideth by,
Frost-pearled are all the boughs in forests old,
The sheep are huddling close upon the wold,
And over them the stars tremble on high.
Pure joys these winter nights around me lie:
'T is fine to loiter through the lighted streets
At Christmas time, and guess from brow and pace
The doom and history of each one we meet,
What kind of heart beats in each dusky case;
Whiles startled by the beauty of a face
In a shop-light a moment. Or instead,
To dream of silent fields where calm and deep
The sunshine lieth like a golden sleep —
Recalling sweetest looks of Summers dead.

NOTICES FROM THE LONDON PRESS.

Most abundant in beauties. Our extracts, which have been chosen chiefly to illustrate our account of the poem, have scarcely shown the poet at his best. Everywhere his poem has lines and phrases revealing a wealth of poetical thought and expression. — *Athenæum.*

Since Tennyson, no poet has come before the public with the same promise as the author of this volume. . . . . There are many lines and sentences in these poems which must become familiar on the lips of lovers of poetry. — *Literary Gazette.*

It is to the earlier works of Keats and Shelley alone that we can look for a counterpart, in richness of fancy and force of expression. . . . . These extracts will induce every lover of true poetry to read the volume for himself; we do not think that, after such reading, any one will be disposed to doubt that Alexander Smith promises to be a greater poet than any emergent genius of the last few years. — *Spectator.*

The most striking characteristic of these poems is their abundant *imagery,* — fresh, vivid, concrete images actually present to the poet's mind, and thrown out with a distinctiveness and a delicacy only poets can achieve. There is not a page of this volume on which we cannot find some novel image, some Shaksperian felicity of expression, or some striking simile. — *Westminster Review.*

Mr. Smith has given noble proof of possessing some of the best attributes of the true poet. One of his special characteristics is a luxuriant imagination, which continually suggests poetical images, and is happily allied to a singular mastery of language in one so young, which enables him to apply them with almost intuitive felicity. Nearly every page is studded with striking metaphors. — *Sunday Times.*

It is seldom that a new work is met with which furnishes such incontestable evidence of the possession of great powers by the author as the present. It is impossible to read three consecutive pages without feeling in the presence of a spirit moved with a profound sense of all forms of spiritual beauty. Mr. Smith's language is, in the purest sense of the word, poetic, — that is, it is not only the very best for the expression of the idea, but is suggestive, — it summons up all the accessories to the idea. It is strong and splendid, like golden armor. — *Daily News.*

We have quoted enough, and yet we have not quoted a third of the fine passages our pencil has marked. Having read these extracts, turn to any poet you will, and compare the texture of the composition, — it is a severe test, but you will find that Alexander Smith bears it well. — *Leader.*

www.ingramcontent.com/pod-product-compliance
Lightning Source LLC
LaVergne TN
LVHW011214110826
845150LV00006B/1431

9781425517007